Please remember that this is a library book,
and that it belongs only temporarily to each
person who uses it. Be considerate. Do
not write in this, or any, library book.

WITHDRAWN

TEACHING AND THE UNCONSCIOUS MIND

TEACHING
and the
UNCONSCIOUS MIND

John C. Hill, M.Sc.

INTERNATIONAL UNIVERSITIES PRESS, INC.
New York

Library of Congress Catalog Card Number: 78-141661

Manufactured in the United States of America

"I have hope that society may be reformed, when I see how much education may be reformed."
—G. W. Leibnitz

Contents

Foreword—Anna Freud   ix

Introduction—Rudolf Ekstein, Ph.D.   1

1   Activity Methods   5

2   Class Management   31

3   The Unconscious Mind   37

4   Early Education   48
     Education in the Home   48
     Nursery Class   59
     Infants School   62
     Junior School   67

5   Secondary Education   75

6   School Subjects   82
     Art   83
     Music and Speech   86
     Composition   91
     Mathematics   95
     Geography   101
     History   104
     Physical Education and Handwork   106

7   Some General Problems   113
     The Marking of Books   113
     Discipline   116

CONTENTS

The Inheritance of Acquired Characters   121
Mind and Intellect   123
Culture   126
The Limitations of the Intellect   129
Educational Therapy   134
Some Further References to
    the Unconscious Mind   139

Appendix   145
    Freud's Influence on Education   145

References   159

Index   163

Foreword

IN THE DISCIPLINE of psychoanalysis we are seeing a growing tendency to concentrate interest on the most recent theoretical advances or on the latest applications of knowledge, and to ignore previous work altogether or regard it almost condescendingly as the clumsy and fumbling efforts of imperfectly equipped pioneers. Unfortunately, publishers and editors fall in with this predilection shown by their reading public and contribute to the neglect of the past by allowing valuable books to run out of print, or valuable articles to remain buried in inaccessible periodicals.

The compilation and publication of this book is, therefore, doubly welcome. As Dr. Ekstein points out in the Introduction, John C. Hill made his first contribution to our subject in the middle of the nineteen twenties, which places him firmly among the pioneers. None of the facilities which educators could turn to in later years for systematic instruction in the new child psychology was available to him. This disadvantageous state of affairs had its advantages, since it left Mr. Hill free to make his own selection of psychoanalytic theorems for application to his field of work. It seems that he went to the heart of the matter when he gave preference to the following principles:

The child's *unconscious mind,* its innate contents as well as its dynamic energies, provides the significant material with which teachers have to deal and which they have to respect.

The *wish to explore* and know, that is, to *learn* on the individual's own terms, is a natural, inborn tendency which needs to be given scope and satisfaction during education and which must not be smothered or submerged by teaching methods which are alien to the child.

The child's *intellect,* his *fantasy,* and his ability for *artistic expression* are equally active in the process of learning and have to be given equal importance in this respect.

The inherited *instincts* have to be checked and *controlled* sufficiently to allow social behavior and sublimated interests to display themselves.

It is always a pleasure to see practice grow out of theory, to see psychoanalytic principles applied to new areas of human life or, as in Mr. Hill's case, to find confirmed in the daily events of school life what has been unearthed laboriously from the repressed childhood memories of analytic patients. By now, the author of the book has long outgrown his activities in schools, classrooms, and teachers' colleges. But, since unusual gifts will never be denied, we can still have the occasional privilege of seeing him in action with individual hesitant learners, performing miracles of teaching and education which can only be brought about on the basis of his own precepts.

London, 1970   Anna Freud

Introduction

RUDOLF EKSTEIN, Ph.D.

During the past decade I have been helping to develop programs through which psychoanalytic insights, reformulated around the issues of learning, may be carried to teachers and educators. In the early years of this endeavor, Dr. Rocco L. Motto and I sent a manuscript to Miss Anna Freud describing the postgraduate activities we had been developing for teachers who were interested in applying psychoanalytic principles to education. Miss Freud responded (in May 1962) as follows:

> Thank you so much for sending me a copy of your paper, "Psychoanalysis and Education—Past and Future." I have read it with great interest, since this is so much also my past. But I was struck by one omission, and I thought you would be interested to hear about it. There are very few people who have actually applied psychoanalysis to classroom teaching. But there is one man here in London who has done so constantly all through his career. After successful experiences in teaching, training teachers, and as a university lecturer, he was appointed inspector of schools for the London County Council, and supervised the schools in a large area of East London. I met him soon after my arrival in London in 1938; and I was amazed at his grasp of psychoanalytic principles and their usefulness for education. His name is Mr. J. C. Hill. I am sending you . . . a list of his publications. . . .

I wrote to Mr. Hill who was kind enough to send me some of his early publications. They began with his paper

[1]

"Poetry and the Unconscious"[57] which appeared in The British Journal of Medical Psychology in 1924, a date which caught my attention because it predated the publication of the English translation of Freud's *The Ego and the Id* (1927).[50] I noticed, too, that Mr. Hill's book, *The Teacher in Training* was published one year prior to the publication of Anna Freud's classic *The Ego and the Mechanisms of Defense* (1936).[29] Clearly, John C. Hill's contributions started at the very beginning of the collaborative venture between psychoanalysis and education.

Coming as they did before the introduction of the concept of the ego, id, and superego, Mr. Hill's early contributions to the literature are written in language characteristic of Freud's earlier concept of the conscious, preconscious, and unconscious. When Mr. Hill speaks about teaching and the unconscious mind, his language may remind us of those earlier times, but his ideas have particular relevance for what goes on in the classroom of today. He gives us just as much theory as is pertinent, because he is always concerned with the practical application of psychoanalytic understanding to the educational process.

Let us consider this, for example, from his *Dreams and Education* (1926):

> Freud is sometimes spoken of by psychoanalysts as "Darwin of the mind." The writer of this book is not a practicing psychoanalyst: he has little experience of abnormal human beings, and on some of Freud's work he is not competent to express an opinion. But he has applied Freud's main hypotheses to the study of normal human conduct, and the results have been so illuminating that he has no hesitation in subscribing to the view that Freud's work is the greatest individual contribution that has ever been made to psychology, and a contribution with which parents and teachers should be acquainted at once.

These are great claims to make for the new psychology and, of course, they have to be proved. Freud and his disciples have tried to prove them and have been met in many quarters with derision. But since several English and American psychologists of high standing have investigated Freud's work and proclaimed the truth of, at least, a great part of it, the problem is receiving serious consideration from educated people. It is this more hopeful atmosphere which encourages the present writer to try to explain to parents and teachers some of the more important aspects of Freud's work.[56]

In 1935, Mr. Hill, having been on the staff of London University for a number of years and having contributed to the training of teachers, published *The Teacher in Training*. In his preface he says:

The child should grow in knowledge as a tree grows, and not as a wall grows, with every brick well and truly laid. The student in training as a teacher should grow in knowledge in the same way. It is hoped that this book will give him some fresh views about education and will help him to gather together his own experiences and the experiences of his tutors and colleagues.[58]

On receiving a copy of this book, Freud wrote Mr. Hill:

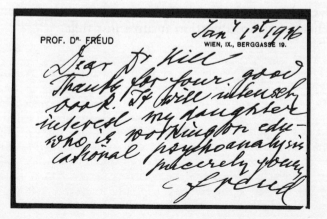

Two years later, Freud was forced to leave Austria and he and his family were made welcome in England. The Professor and Anna Freud were given a fresh opportunity to speak out for psychoanalysis. Miss Freud, for her first public address in the fall of 1938, chose to give a group of lectures directed to teachers. The man who invited her, who organized the meeting, and who chaired it, was John C. Hill. I attended those meetings.

Although Mr. Hill and I have been associated with the same enterprise throughout these many years, we met only after 1962, when, at our invitation, he came to Los Angeles to address our teachers. Some of his work has subsequently been published in the *Reiss-Davis Clinic Bulletin,* and his articles appear regularly in *The London Head Teacher.* Many of these articles are included in this new book which I have the privilege of introducing. Mr. Hill's work symbolizes our fruitful past, our work today, and our dedication to a new creative era in the collaboration between education and psychoanalysis. I am delighted to know it will be available to young teachers in all English-speaking countries. How can one possibly envisage public education in free countries unless there also exists a deep interest in the individual? The contribution of psychoanalysis to education insures just that.

Chapter One

Activity Methods

IN 1930 I WAS appointed an Inspector of Schools for the London County Council, and sent to supervise the schools in Bethnal Green, Bow, Bromley and Poplar in the East End of London. I was first of all impressed with the excellent work being done in most of the infants schools. Many of the children came in at three years of age and although the classes were seldom less than forty pupils, the children were well cared for and were trained and educated in a kindly way. Many of them preferred the school life to the holiday periods. Almost all the children could read, write, and count when they went to the junior school at nearly eight years of age and many had a much broader education than this. I was particularly impressed by some of the original compositions—this kind of thing, for example, by a seven-and-a-half-year-old.

When I Grow Up

Would you like to know about when I grow up? I am going to be a char-a-banc driver and I am going to charge a lot of money to go to Ramsgate and Broadstairs and then we will come home and I will take the char-a-banc to the garage. And I will get up early in the morning and go and get the char-a-banc and go to Hastings. It will be lovely to go again. We saw some pigs and

[5]

some sheep and we saw lots of horses and we saw a man cleaning an aeroplane and we have to go home to have our tea and then we go to the sands and we have ice cream cornet and then we make sand castles and then go home. And in the morning we have our breakfast we have a very nice breakfast and then we get our spades and go in sand to make a deep hole in the sand and we do have a lovely time and then we go and get the char-a-banc and go again to Ramsgate and Broadstairs and Hastings and then we go home and get to bed and go asleep.

There are mistakes in punctuation of course, but the big things are right, and the result is worth reading. The teachers were very sparing with their criticism, although they did give guidance, and they never defaced the child's work with red ink, blue pencil, or scribbled comments. As the marking therefore took little time, the pupils were allowed to write freely almost every day.

In so many of these infants schools there was a happy family atmosphere. The needs of the children had evoked the maternal instinct in many of the teachers and the gratitude of the overworked East End mothers was a further encouragement to them. The junior schools, on the other hand, were not as a rule so interesting. The work there was usually more formal, and while there were some excellent teachers, I felt that if the infants methods could be carried forward into the junior schools, the education would be much better. Every error in the compositions was usually corrected in red ink and every set of free compositions took the teacher two hours to correct. The result was that the children were only allowed to write original work about once a week.

I suggested to some of the junior Heads that they should let the children write more often and correct as the infants teachers did, namely giving a few corrections verbally or in soft lead pencil, and not defacing the child's original work with red ink or scribbled comments; treat the child's original composition as one would treat a colleague's manuscript. This was heresy to some Heads. I was asked at a meeting of headteachers what they were to do when the Council's inspector told them not to correct all errors, and the Ministry's inspector would complain if all errors in the compositions were not corrected. I said, "Pay no attention to either of them. The Head of of the school is captain of the ship. He should do what he thinks right for his school and not take orders from any inspector." I added that this was the policy of both the Board of Education and the London County Council. Inspectors give advice to headteachers on educational matters, not orders.

The air being cleared, several teachers tried the infants procedure, and were surprised to find that spelling and punctuation improved in some curious way without detailed correction. These experimenters were, of course, skilled class teachers. If a student from the training college tried this method to begin with he would probably find the composition would get steadily worse. There is an important unconscious mind factor in this work which we shall explain later.

Miss Marion Richardson had been appointed inspector for art work about the same time as I was appointed. The remarkable success of her free approach in art teaching made quite a sensation in East London schools. I arranged an Open Day at the first school in East London in which Miss Richardson had been introducing her methods—a school of four hundred infants in Bethnal Green. There were over one hundred visitors, including the late Mr. Roger Fry. This is his description of the visit, published in *The New Statesman and Nation* the following week (June 24th, 1933).

It is an extraordinary sight to see the children from the drabbest slums of the East End painting away at these designs which they have made without any help. Their passionate concentration is unbelievable unless seen. They grudge every moment of the rest intervals and rush back to work, and the mothers complain that they linger on long after school hours. Nor need the visitor fear to disturb them at their work for they never look up and hardly deign to answer if spoken to.

Now what is so extraordinary about these works is that among the hundreds and hundreds that I have seen, I have hardly ever seen a single colour discord, and I have seen such subtle and un-expected felicities as make an artist feel a pang of envy. And yet one has only to look at a book of wallpaper patterns or of sample decorator's colours to know that the average adult Englishman has as much idea of colour as an old boot.

This is surely an interesting discovery. It suggests that the har-monies accepted by artists correspond to some fundamental, nat-ural, instinctive reaction, but that our education and the traditions and examples of modern civilization always distort it so that the artist's job is, as in so many things, merely to get back to the simplest, most immediate and native reaction. Many of the designs which come from these infant schools might be translated into the most beautiful textiles with only the slightest adjustment and ar-rangement, and they certainly would refresh our jaded industrial art with some delightful and unexpected discoveries.

More teachers began to experiment with free methods in a variety of school subjects, and soon some quite re-markable results were obtained. In 1948 I was asked to give four lectures on junior school methods to London teachers, and of course, I referred to recent developments. There was a large audience and I was asked to repeat the lectures the following year. I decided instead to invite teachers to visit four East London junior schools in which these new methods were used. The children would be given the afternoon off, and brought to school in the

[8]

evening so that visitors could see what was being done, and judge the results.

The junior school at Atley Road, Bow, was one of the four chosen. Mrs. Catherine Howlett was the headmistress and she gave an explanatory talk to the visitors. Although it was given many years ago, it is still quite up-to-date, and is one of the best descriptions I have seen of how to introduce Activity Methods and develop them. She has very kindly allowed me to reproduce her talk, substantially as she gave it.

"Whether a teacher teaches by Activity Methods or by more formal methods, the measure of his success in his job is determined by the sincerity with which he puts his children's needs first. If he can say that his children are spontaneous, interested, want to work, that each child is developing happily and to the best of his ability, that there is an affectionate intimacy between his children and himself, that they are beginning to respond to an inner discipline and are mastering the art of getting on well with their fellows, then no matter what methods the teacher uses, he is on the right track. If he knows that what the junior child wants of school is hard work, adventure, and the enjoyment that comes from a feeling of successful achievement, then he will not go far wrong. And here it is as well to say that no matter how good a teacher is in teaching subject matter, it is often the quiet word spoken at an odd time to the individual child, the mutual appreciation of a good joke, the sympathetic inquiry about a sick mother, or the sharing of an exciting interest in a new baby that leaves a lasting impression. In other words, be yourself—free, spontaneous, and happy, and your children will be also.

"No child or adult can be free, spontaneous, and happy

if he is afraid. It has been said that *fear* and *interest* are the two dominant colors, either of which may emerge in the life pattern of a child. This pattern he works out for himself as a result of his inheritance and his experiences, and to this design his parents, teachers, schoolfellows, and his surroundings all contribute. If the pattern which emerges is fear, a child's attitude is one of holding back and he lives in a state of tension. In effect, he assumes that what is strange is dangerous, and being ashamed of his fear he tries to assert his superiority—hence he is aggressive and difficult and incapable of working with ease or enjoyment. He becomes afraid of failure most often because he has been given things to do for which he was not ready and because he has been ridiculed and punished when he failed. Punishment in one form or another piles fear on fear. Maladjustment may result and he grows into an adult who cannot fit into a community or get on with his fellows. Experienced teachers will recognize here the child that sometimes developed under the old, regimented school discipline where all the children were being molded into the same pattern, where teachers were so busy instilling facts which might or might not be useful in other or future situations, and keeping so rigidly to a cramped timetable they had no time to understand the children or their individual needs. By using Activity Methods of teaching we believe we are making a child's pattern of living an interest pattern, so that his attitude is that of welcoming fresh experiences and new adventures. Such children are at ease with themselves and are not afraid to feel and think for themselves. But everything depends on the relationship between teacher and child; whatever aspect of education we take, or at whatever stage, the relationship between teacher and child is the all-important factor. The growth of confidence, the elimination of fear, mutual love and understanding—these are the elements with which a teacher must work.

"As a headteacher I do not believe that teachers should be directed in so many words to use Activity Methods. The success of their use depends primarily on the sincerity of the teacher, her belief in their value, her enthusiasm, and her capacity to undertake what is a far harder job than any formal instruction. In my opinion it takes a first-class teacher to use these methods properly. Many teachers can nibble at them, but it is the exceptional teacher who can go all the way. It is no wonder that older teachers, themselves brought up under an academic tradition, find it well-nigh impossible to throw overboard the ideas of a lifetime, to realize that it is not the time spent in teaching subject matter that is important, but the time spent in helping children to acquire useful attitudes to learning that is important. Ironically enough, these teachers are the very people who, once they take the plunge, are the best exponents of the new methods. They have at their fingertips the easiness of class control, they know what standards of work are possible for a child to achieve happily, they have a wide background of knowledge, and they have come to have an understanding of their children. And here a word to the young teacher just out of college: teach through formal methods first, get your class control, learn to know your children, give yourself time to realize the different standards that are possible in what I would call the skills; reading, writing, and arithmetic. Then when you feel happily confident, begin to use Activity Methods if you want to, but begin slowly and move slowly.

"No teacher in this school is compelled to use Activity Methods. What has happened is that one or two teachers experimented with them, found them successful, and their enthusiasm carried them on to more difficult work. Their successes stimulated other teachers to attempt Activity Methods, and they too, retained those methods which brought *them* success. I would like to say here that the teachers themselves are a fine example to the children in that they are always willing to help one another and share their ideas. Children and teachers talk of their work together, share thoughts, enthusiasms, pictures, books, and so learn from each other. This I contend is one of the happiest results of using Activity Methods in school; no self-centered child or adult could hope to take part successfully in such a rich communal life. Whatever Activity Methods our teachers use, they are fully aware of one fundamental point; the reason for using Activity Methods is to enable children to learn by doing and if in that doing the child learns nothing, then the activity is a waste of time. Teachers are also aware that the use of Activity Methods involves more than handwork. The wise teacher watches her opportunity and uses speech, miming, written work, simple research, painting, exploratory walks, education visits, the film strip, the moving film. There is no set method of teaching through Activity Methods, but there must be an aim, there must be a reason for the activity. The activity should be a means of learning and not an end in itself.

"Each child in most classes has three loose-leaf notebooks in which he writes his original notes after history, geography, and science lessons. The two lower backward classes have one expression workbook in which all are combined. These books are illustrated by drawings and pictures which the children have collected themselves. Some of the notes are full and good, others poor and scrappy, but if the most backward child has gleaned one thing of interest and put it down and found for himself a picture to put beside it, then he has accomplished something in which to take pride. These books pass up with the child through the school. A boy can turn back and see what he did when he was eight and compare it with his achievements at 11 plus. I have watched boys swapping pictures in the playground and often I have seen a boy nudge his neighbor and whilst pointing to a back page, heard him say, 'Look at that!—and this!' as he turns to a more recent piece of work. This progression which a child can see at a glance is encouraging and the children are proud of their books and keen to take them home when they leave. Incidentally, these notebooks, together with their record books in which the children file a monthly test in English and arithmetic, provide the interviewing Head of the secondary school with a very good idea of the children's ability.

"Last year teachers in classes 1A, 1B, and 2A* began a most valuable activity. To encourage the children to find out things for themselves, they suggested that each child should compile an *individual book*. After discussions with their teachers the children chose their own subjects. Photography, Birds and Bird Watching, Animals, Explorers, Sports of the World, Flowers, Transport, Fish, Docks, Kings and Queens, Ships, Reptiles, The Royal Family, The Ballet, and Bible stories are just a few. The writing of these books had nothing to do with the teacher except that a child could ask for help and guidance. The children found they needed books for reference, therefore

---

* *Author's Note:* A, B, and C are three "streams" of pupils, the "A" stream being the brightest pupils, and the "C" stream the most backward. Class 1A consisted of the brightest fourth-year pupils (aged 10–11 plus), Class 2A consisted of the brightest third-year pupils (aged nine–10), Class 3A consisted of the brightest second-year pupils (aged eight–nine), and Class 4A consisted of the brightest first-year pupils (aged seven–eight). Pupils change from the Infants Department to the Junior Department between the ages of seven and eight.

they needed to join the library. We are lucky in having two public libraries close at hand. Each class has a class library and we have a children's school reference library. One of the first things we noticed was the striking interest the parents showed in the children's work, for the work was done at home as well as in school. Fathers took their boys for educational visits on Saturday afternoons—to the docks, museums, and places of historical interest, and bought them postcards to illustrate their subject matter. From this activity the children learned to select books from the library, to differentiate between the important and the unimportant, to use new words, to use a dictionary, and they gained a sense of achievement in the compilation of a book of their very own. Their subjects this year include Peoples of the World, Astronomy, The Capital Cities of the World, Snakes and Monkeys, Great Football Teams, Airplanes and Rockets, Living Things, Wonders of the World, Places and History in London.

"The lower classes of the school are not yet ready for such an ambitious project. They are still striving to get fluency in written English and to encourage this, all children in the middle and lower school write a *daily diary*. From these diaries we get glimpses of homelife which contribute to our understanding of the children. At the very bottom of the school, where we have a little class of 28 children all about eight years of age and all struggling with the mechanics of reading, this daily free writing is invaluable. In this class the teacher doesn't call it 'writing in your diary' but 'writing a story.' The beginning of the book is often just scribble and then when an attempt is made to write words, they are illegible. Very slowly the writing becomes legible and one day the teacher can read it to the class and soon everybody is trying to write a story teacher can read. I have seen a teacher surrounded by eager children each asking how to spell a word. The point I want to make here is that these children have lost the apathy which often accompanies backwardness and are eager and keen to learn. In all learning there should be a motive for learning; in this case the child wants his teacher to be able to read his story and so he must write it well. The teacher in this lowest class continues with infant methods using command cards, cutout letters for word building, simple jigsaw puzzles containing words and pictures, and the children have made themselves a large *wall dictionary* using large sheets of sugar paper and many pictures which they themselves have collected. Another class in the lower part of the school has made team pictorial dictionaries, each child having made himself responsible for one page of the dictionary.

"I have always believed that a child should be able to see and measure his progress, on the principle that nothing succeeds like success. Periodically, I test all the children on the 'B' side of the school using a standard reading test. I tell them how much progress they have made in a given time and write this on a small piece of paper which they take home. The eagerness with which the children await their turn to come singly up to my room has to be seen to be believed; no child is frightened, we have turned it into a kind of game. Every day I am asked, 'When are you going to hear me read?' Many of the parents interested in the tests now spend a little time each evening helping their youngsters learn to read. This testing and praising of the smallest effort has paid rich dividends and the teachers have told me that they like to measure the success of their work in this way. Because the children feel thoroughly at home with me during the test, intimate and amusing conversations take place. I remember the little girl who stumbled over the word 'wine.' I asked her if she knew what wine was. 'Oh yes,' said she, 'it's in bottles and my Nan has a pint every Saturday night.' I remember too, the small boy who reached the third page of the test for the first time. Heaving a sigh of happy relief at having accomplished so much, he cast an anxious eye at the more difficult words on the new page. 'Oh Lord,' he gasped, 'I'll never get down *this* page!' I want to emphasize here that I thoroughly enjoy the taking of these tests and I think the children do too; but the right, friendly, intimate, atmosphere is essential to their success.

"We want our children to speak clearly and confidently. Every morning during assembly we have a passage read from the Bible by a child who has practiced reading it beforehand. Classes take it in turn to read week by week and any child who wishes to do so and is considered by his teacher to be good enough, may read to the school. In this way the children perceive a good standard of reading toward which they may strive, acquire confidence in standing before a large number of people, and perhaps learn to appreciate the modulation of good speaking voices; I have seen the whole school hushed and spellbound by a child's beautifully modulated voice. 'Can I read at prayer time?' is a frequent question and one of the most satisfying feelings I have known is that which comes to a teacher of a child who only a very short time ago was in the remove class* at the bottom of the school, unable to read at all, who one day acquits himself creditably by reading to the school.

"Every year we have a Verse Speaking Afternoon when classes assemble in the hall and speak their poems or prose from the Bible to the school. This may include choral

---

* *Author's Note:* This is only a polite name for a small class of the most backward children who came up from the Infants Department at not quite eight years of age and needed special teaching.

work or individual speech work. Each class has a weekly period for *dramatic work* which may take various forms. All children delight in spontaneously acting their own stories and in this kind of dramatic work the leaders and born organizers of the class shine, but the puppet play is a help to the shy child; where faces are hidden there is little self-consciousness. Younger children have made flat, cardboard puppets. Children of 3B held a discussion with their teacher and found the answers to these questions: who will collect the old stockings to make the puppet heads; who will sew the stuffed heads and paint the faces; collect the odd pieces of material and sew the dresses; write the play; speak the different parts; paint the scenery? This became the basis for an activity lesson and soon the class was to be seen divided into groups, each getting on with its own job. My next view of the proceedings was watching different children trying out the parts in Cinderella. To my adult eyes, Cinderella the puppet was no better looking than her ugly sisters, but the children were completely satisfied and enthralled as they watched their companions operate the puppets and heard their attempts at speaking the parts. Last Christmas, Class 1A produced a nativity play. The usual discussion took place and different jobs were found for different groups; the painting of the scenery, collection of dresses, singing of carols or solos, the speaking of parts from the Bible, miming of the shepherds, angels, wisemen. The whole class participated. I want to emphasize that this activity did not begin until a fortnight before Christmas. We do not aim at a finished performance but want the natural spontaneity of the children, so much so that each rehearsal produced something different, just as the children felt at the time.

"All teachers use the medium of *dramatic work* for free expression of their *history lessons*. We have an annual

History Afternoon when the children in each class, having selected material from a history lesson which they wish to mime, present the mime to the school. Before the performance, the subject matter is broken up into small scenes and then briefly written out by the children. Each mime is preceded by the reading of its meaning so that the whole audience, young and old, has some assurance of understanding what the little mime is all about. Here are the stories that were mimed on our last History Afternoon: The Lady of the Pyramids, a story of Ancient Egypt, by 4A; The Slaves of Rameses, by 4B; Princess Dido and the Founding of Carthage, by 3B; The Writing on the Wall at Belshazzar's Feast, by 3A; St. George and the Dragon, by remove; The Burghers of Calais, by 2A; Sir Walter Raleigh, by 2B; Elizabeth Fry, by 1B; and William Penn, by 1A.

"I shall remember several episodes in the miming for a long time, and so will the children. Raleigh's sea battle with the Spaniards, the ramming of the powder in the guns, applying the match to the touch hole, and the falling back of the sailors as the guns recoiled, are not easily forgotten. Nor is a later scene in which Raleigh, interrupted in his writing of the History of the World, was solemnly bound about the wrists and marched off to his execution with a truly impressive body of guards. And who of us who witnessed the great feast of Belshazzar, waving fans borne by slaves, will forget the slow appearance inside a classroom door window of a sign bearing the pregnant words, 'Mene, Mene, Tekel, Upharsin,' which was followed by a perfectly riotous and thoroughly enjoyed battle. And class 1B scored a triumph in the presentation of Elizabeth Fry. It was, for a children's production, moving in its simplicity. The opening scene was quite terrible with its tousled, quarrelling women and their sobbing children. The difference in the atmosphere in the second scene, which took

[18]

place after Elizabeth Fry's work, was well brought out; we saw the women tending their children, cutting out and sewing clothes, listening to a Bible reading, saying prayers, and singing hymns, with Elizabeth Fry giving them the note like a Presbyterian precentor. All this was thoroughly enjoyed by actors and audience and I am sure the dramatic presentation of these history stories by the children themselves will be an abiding memory.

"This year the teachers of classes 1A, 2B, 3A, and 3C combined their history, geography, and science lessons into what we call environmental and social studies. Children of class 3C took as their starting point, The House, while 3A started with their own neighborhood of Poplar. Class 2B took London and its relation to England and 1A took England as the first stop in journeys around the world. This last class did not include science as the children were interested in a course of lessons on the wireless on 'How Things Began.' In class 1A the project was begun after the children heard a broadcast of 'Susannah of the Mounties.' They were interested in Canada and suggested that they pay an imaginary visit there. Some children brought air travel pamphlets, others wrote to the airlines for material.

"Whilst waiting for replies, and during a general talk about America, one child who had been reading a book from the children's reference library, disputed the statement that Columbus discovered America. He told the class what he had read about the Vikings discovering America. This was followed by another child bringing a newspaper article describing the unveiling of a statue of John Cabot, in Bristol. The teacher seized this point of interest and followed it up by reading extracts describing Labrador and Greenland from a travel book she had been reading entitled *I Married an Adventurer*. Soon after, eager chil-

[19]

dren told of seeing 'Meet the Huskies' on television, which had been followed by scenes of the Canadian Mounties. The teacher then introduced the maple tree and maple syrup. Some of the boys brought pictures of Canadian trains and the children drew the routes of the C.P.R. across the continent. The teacher again brought in her own reading and read extracts from a modern book, *Wasa, Wasa,* giving vivid descriptions of the moose and elk, climatic conditions, and the work of fur trappers. The children showed great concern about how these people got on with the Indians, so the teacher switched from Canada and told the story of William Penn and introduced the children to *The Last of the Mohicans.*

"By now, information had arrived from the airlines, so the class went on an air trip to Canada. They drew maps and wrote something about the journey; each child being either a pilot, a hostess, or a passenger. At this time the teacher started a history of flying. Then she told how people had settled in America; the French in Canada, the English in the New England states, and the Spanish in the southern states. At the same time, one boy told the class of Jacques Cartier exploring the St. Lawrence River. The teacher followed up with stories of Wolfe and Quebec, the settlers with Sir Walter Raleigh and Sir Humphrey Gilbert, and the Mayflower and Massachusetts. This was linked with Thanksgiving Day and the harvest and was followed by the War of Independence and Washington as the first president.

"In dealing with the opening of the West, the teacher read extracts from her own reading of that old book of 1846, *The Oregon Trail.* The children were thrilled and in their writing each pretended to be a person going on the trail, the leader or a son or a scout. Some described the assembly of wagons at that last outpost of civilization,

Westport, and one lad made all his characters boys in his class. The children were really living this experience in imagination. Models were constructed and backgrounds painted to illustrate lessons; one showed the ice cap in Greenland and another, the covered wagons ready for an Indian attack. The teachers encouraged each child to make something worthy of inclusion in the large travel book, and in the end, all the children made a contribution. They also have some record of the project in their own note-books.

"You will have noticed that most of this work arose from the children's curiosity which the teacher helped them to satisfy, and that when the impetus from the children seemed likely to stop, she guided them to a new path. No set textbook was used. The children's individual reading often provided the starting point and the teacher aroused their enthusiasm by sharing her pleasure in her own reading. You will, of course, have noticed too, that historical events were often not in their proper chronological order and that in the study of a continent the children seemed to leap from place to place. No detailed study should be attempted at this age; it is enough to use the natural curiosity of the child. When he writes about something, or models something which is of absorbing interest to him, he also perfects the tools *he* uses; his English, his writing, and his craftsmanhip. Lessons take on a different meaning to the child if *he* has introduced the subject, if *he* has found the book, if *he* heard the story on the wireless or saw it on the television.

"Comparing notes with the teacher of 1A, the teacher of 2B found that his children had not the sustained interest of the brighter children. The impetus from the children stopped more often and he had to guide them more frequently. Often he did this with the use of strip and moving films. Nevertheless, it is his considered opinion that he has covered more ground in an interesting and stimulating way, both for the children and himself, than he would have done in formal lessons. The first question from the children was, 'Which is the River Lea and which the canal?'—this in the immediate neighborhood of the school. This led to a lesson on canals and rivers and the position of London was plotted on the Thames, also of Essex which can be seen from the school windows. The children followed this up by talking of Southend and other holiday places. These were fixed on the map and approximate distances from London worked out from the map. Following a natural sequence, the teacher talked about modes of travel used to reach these places which, in turn, led quite easily into the history of transport. In his science lessons he gave simple talks on water, steam and power, and the relation of weight to strength in solid and spoked wheels.

"The history of transport was bound up with the history of roads, and the children learned of Roman roads, of Telford, McAdam, highwaymen, linkmen, sedan chairs, and toll houses. Before visiting the Tower they learned something of its history, and whilst standing on Tower Bridge began to understand the importance of the Thames as a waterway. One child asked what the source of the Thames looked like and the teacher responded with a lesson on springs. Another said, 'I thought you said water couldn't go up—it must always fall down.' The teacher seized his opportunity and gave a modest lesson on water pressure and artesian wells. The children learned that the fountains in Trafalgar Square had once been artesian but were now worked by electricity. Locks and weirs were spoken of and the children paid a visit to Old Ford Lock where they saw the barges passing through the lock gates.

[22]

A river film introduced docks. They located Southampton, Liverpool, Hull, Glasgow, and Belfast on a map. They followed this with simple research, bringing to school lists of articles at home and in shops that had come to us through the docks. These were collated on the blackboard, drawings were made of the articles, and the names of their countries of origin were written below. A film strip, 'London to Birmingham by Canal,' showed the cargoes of barges and this led to the Birmingham steel industry. Again, lists of articles were brought to school, but this time those made from iron and steel were mentioned. The children learned of steelmaking and of the accidental discovery of stainless steel. They conducted their own experiments, scraping the tin from a tin can and learning that iron exposed to air rusts more quickly when the tin is scraped off. They made models of early cavemen pushing blocks of stones on rollers, models of wagons on wheels, sedan chairs, the rocket engine, and motor lorries. Each child wrote his own notes in his own file and the teacher encouraged as many as possible to contribute to the class book. Two boys whose serious backwardness had caused concern contributed two very creditable drawings whilst two other retarded children painted the patterns with which the book was decorated. At present, the children are interested in the bringing of home-produced food to the London markets: Covent Garden, Billingsgate, Smithfield, and Leadenhall.

"Here is a description of an actual activity lesson taken in connection with social studies lessons. Class 3A had been talking of barges carrying timber up the River Lea. They had been hearing of Roman settlements in Bow. In this lesson the children split into groups and each set to work on a special job. One group painted a large map of Canada showing where the timber came from, another was busy cutting stenciled outlines of animals and people to put on the map, while a third was engrossed in drawing pictures of log cabins and trees. The fourth group was occupied in making a log cabin from cardboard, whilst the fifth was manipulating Plasticine into imitation Roman pottery. Yet another group was constructing a model of a Roman villa from cardboard and last of all, a few children were still writing their notes. You will see that every one of these activities had an actual bearing on the lesson and that the children were learning through doing.

"In teaching arithmetic we use concrete methods, especially on the 'B' side of the school. Each child in the remove class has a small box in which he keeps twenty buttons, beans, or even small stones, and uses them as counters. He also uses one inch cubes to build up his tables. Older children equipped with a bath of water, quart and pint bottles, and a gallon can, enjoy finding out, by seeing, how many pint bottles fill a gallon can. Even the dullest boy enjoys weighing sand on scales in order to discover how many ounces make a quarter of a pound, a half of a pound, and so on. Older children have made cardboard clocks in handwork lessons, for the use of the younger ones. At the top of the school, children using laths a yard in length, with each foot painted a different color, enjoy practical measuration lessons in the playground, finding the answers to those tricky irregular area sums and later drawing their measurements to scale. They also like having a free hand with one inch cubes, building up cubes of various sizes, drawing them, and finding cubic capacity which they can see at a glance. One master, teaching the finding of irregular areas to class 2B, has drawn various irregular figures on cardboard and his children delight in covering the figures with one inch squares and then easily counting the area in square inches. He also evolved a kind of slide rule to obtain the answers to multiplication tables. The child builds up his own tables using cubes and then checks his answer with the slide rule.

"And now I come to what I consider one of our most successful projects. One afternoon about a dozen boys in 1A were let loose in the reference library. The teacher became aware of their interest in the solar system when they asked if they might make a book on astronomy. I think this happened after many of them had seen the film, 'When Worlds Collide.' Each child took a different subject: The Moon, The Planets, The Sun, Gravitation, The Tides. Each did his own research and brought his finished piece of work to his teacher for help and correction. Pictures were found and drawn and the book made. Now came, what was to me, the most surprising outcome of this activity. The boys asked if they could give lectures on these subjects to their own class and also to 2A. A letter of invitation was written and accepted by letter from 2A. The teacher of 1A gave a little talk on how a public meeting is run. A chairman was appointed and all the lecturers were fitted, at their own suggestion, with high sounding names such as Dr. Bookman, Professor Hardy, the Right Honorable Robin Crafer.

"At the appointed time, the chairman made the introductory speech and introduced the various speakers, to the manner born. Each child had practiced reading his speech aloud with emphasis on important points and pauses at appropriate moments. After all the papers had been read the chairman threw the meeting open for discussion and invited questions. Questions there were, for a whole half-hour. There was no trace of self-consciousness on the part of the questioners or the lecturers. I would not have believed it, had I not seen it. The children had to speak clearly, they had to think clearly, and the lecturers had to make use of what they had read and learned in order to answer well. They had to think quickly, too. I was astonished at the knowledge they had gained in their research and at their composure when asked a difficult question. The questioners were not always satisfied and there were many well conducted arguments. This activity gave the children practice in using books for research, practice in picking out important points, practice in speaking in front of a large audience, practice in quick thinking, practice in putting knowledge to use in answering questions. They had also learned the procedure of a public meeting and had greatly extended their vocabulary. They could, and did, use words like 'nebulae—constellations—gravity—planets—asteroids—meteors.' If a teacher had stood in front of a class and taught this subject matter, the children would have remembered little of it, but by using this playway, the whole experience was alive to them.

"On the day of the General Election we held a mock election in which the whole of the fourth year took part. It all arose from a Scripture lesson about the laborers in the vineyard. The meaning of the laborers and labor was discussed, and from there it was a short step to the coming election. How was an election run? What was it for? The teacher said they could have an election themselves and a week before it was to take place the children nominated three candidates. Each candidate, with the teacher's help, wrote his election speech. One candidate stood for the Progressive Party and advocated rocket communication with the planets. Another stood for the Welfare Party and argued that there be more nurses, longer holidays for children, and that teachers should take children on holidays. The third candidate—Independent—wanted to see the Severn tides harnessed for electrical power. Whilst the speeches were being written the rest of the children

[26]

painted posters urging the electorate to cast their votes for the different candidates; they also prepared and cut up paper for voting slips.

"One afternoon we listened to the election speeches. Then the fun really started. The candidates were bombarded with questions and the chairman often had to use his home-made gavel to restore order. We teachers sat back and let the children control the whole meeting. We were astonished at the self-confidence of the chairman, candidates, and questioners. The children's speech was generally clear and where it was not, the chairman, with great aplomb, just said, 'Would the gentleman mind repeating the question? We did not quite catch what he said.' One listener objected to teachers taking children on holiday. When were the poor teachers going to get their holiday? Another said, 'Only the teachers can get the children to behave nicely.' The candidate responded quickly 'It is the parents' job to train the children at home to behave well.' Loud applause from the teachers! Then came the actual voting and we used the puppet theater for the polling booth and a pail covered with a sheet of paper with a slit in it for the ballot box. Children acted as policemen and as polling clerks. There was a presiding officer and blind people were escorted to the polling booth. It was remarkable how many blind voters there were. The children thoroughly enjoyed this activity, especially the cheering when the result of the election was declared next day. It had all been a great adventure. They had again extended their vocabularies, written speeches, painted posters, learned the form of a public meeting, thought of questions and answers, practiced speaking aloud, and had gained some knowledge of how Parliament is constituted.

"We have a school choir. The members are drawn from the middle and upper school after a voice test for which the children consistently volunteer. At morning assemblies the choir is of great value in giving a strong lead to the school and in providing innumerable solo singers; every morning I am bombarded with the same request, 'Can I sing a solo?' Our children are not self-conscious about singing alone once they know they really can sing well. We only recently discovered that a boy who was one of our biggest nuisances and who always wanted to be in the limelight, sang like an angel. He flushed with pleasure at our praise of his singing and his teacher tells me that having asserted his superiority in the right direction, his academic work has improved remarkably.

"We have a recorder class which has accompanied the choir at morning assemblies and one boy taught himself 'We Three Kings' especially for the nativity play. Musical appreciation has its place in our music lessons and often the children will ask if they may illustrate a musical theme in their art lessons. They have painted pictures of the 'Sleeping Princess,' 'Greensleeves,' the fairies of *A Midsummer Night's Dream*, the 'Elf King,' 'Peer Gynt,' the 'Danse Macabre,' and some children have contributed written work to the music magazine.

"I have made no mention of other projects, such as The Holiday Book by 2A, The Appreciation of Library Books by 1B, The Book of Original Poems, the series of models on 'How Things Began' made by last year's 1A. These projects remind us that there is also a great deal of formal work done in this school. The basic subjects, reading, writing, and arithmetic, are all things that need doing whether one feels in the mood for them or not. A child has to learn to face up to the difficult things of life and must put forth his whole effort, but if by using Activity Methods of teaching and learning, we can get 'drive'— the impetus from the child himself—it is a far better way than by dragooning him into doing something in which he is not interested and of which he will retain little. And it all comes back to the relationship between teacher and child. I will say again that the use of Activity Methods of teaching and learning is just not possible without mutual affection and respect between teacher and child, and without the wholehearted giving of the teacher's free, spontaneous self. I believe that in this happy atmosphere we are making progress in education. We are giving the conditions necessary for the development of a child's ability to get on well with his fellows and so preparing him for social contacts which, when he grows up, will be far more varied than his parents ever knew. We are eliminating fear through affection and understanding, developing a growth of confidence, helping personalities to flower, and encouraging all, the bright and the dull, to find happiness in doing a job, each to the best of his ability, be that ability great or small."

Excellent as these methods are, they are not a standard from which other schools should copy in detail. The good schools become good in their own way, depending on the interests of the children and the teachers. Other good schools have art work of a high standard, interesting projects, remarkable puppetry and so on, as well as original notebooks. Original notebooks are essential. The children can all write at once, they cannot all talk at once or make models at once, and they must have some form of expression which is practicable. The essential point is that the *inherited* knowledge and skill of the pupils must be evoked and developed, for intellectual processes without this instinctual support are feeble things. Man, as well as the animals, has a rich instinctual life and most human power comes from a sublimation of this inheritance. In other words, the unconscious mind is much more powerful than the conscious mind.

The sad thing about excellent work of the kind described by Mrs. Howlett is that it may not last in the school which developed it. There are changes of staff, and even excellent Heads have to retire at 65. Their places are often taken by Heads who do not understand the unconscious mind, and the education gradually changes back to a more formal type. There is, of course, more freedom in junior schools now than there used to be, but care must be taken that this does not lead to unsatisfactory discipline and a lower standard of attainment. The pioneers who began free methods and achieved such remarkable success with them were already experienced teachers on formal methods. They had acquired good technical skill in handling and teaching a class of forty pupils. They moved *gradually* into freer methods and had always a safe background to fall back on if anything went wrong. Many young teachers nowadays have no safe background to fall back on, and if they begin with free methods in large classes things can go wrong for them quite frequently.

Technical skill in teaching is not valued so highly now as it used to be. It was a condition of admission to the three year course of training at Glasgow University in my time, that the student should have done at least six months full-time teaching practice before he began the course, and he had to do a good deal more during his three years training. Owing to changed conditions, few present-day students get enough practice in handling a class, and it is generally agreed that they should have some supervision and guidance after they join a school so that they do not fall into bad habits of teaching because of early struggles with class management.

Chapter Two

Class Management

ONE OF THE HALLMARKS of the first-class teacher is the way he uses his eyes. If a young man is talking to two girl friends, he usually knows it is important to look at both of them, if he wants to retain the two friendships. But not one teacher in 10 looks at all the pupils while he is talking to them. A first-class teacher looks at every pupil as he says almost every sentence. If he asks a question from the class, he does not accept an answer immediately; he pauses for two or three seconds and looks again at every pupil. His eyes say, as it were, 'Good, Tom, Dick, Harry—I see you know. You don't know this, do you John, James, Peter—Well, Paul, what do you say?" And everybody is happy. The third-class teacher takes one answer without looking at the other children and they feel neglected. If they are interested in the lesson, they call out, "Please, sir!"; they snap their fingers, or move out closer to the teacher in the hope of attracting his attention, and all they get is, "I told you not to call out." "All right," thinks the boy, "you'll wait a long time before I try to answer again," and soon the pupils have lost interest in the lesson and are getting into mischief.

This attention to each individual is not so necessary,

of course, for university lecturers. In fact, a good teacher changing over to university lecturing, should lose his good eye to some extent. There are often one or two loving couples sitting at the back who are more interested in each other than in the lecture, and some tired individuals who are always looking at their watches. One of my university colleagues said he did not mind a student looking at his watch, he was accustomed to that, but he still hated to see him shake it, thinking it must have stopped. It is usually better for the lecturer to ignore such details and continue to present his lecture in a methodical way. This is one of the reasons why lecturers in education should have been *good* teachers, for only a good teacher knows the importance of technical skill in teaching children.

Another hallmark of the first-class teacher is his silence when the children are reading or writing. When he speaks the children listen. The third-class teacher's voice disturbs the peace of the classroom even when the children are quiet. "Smith! get on with your work—Yes, you would put a blot on it—I told you before to leave a margin." "Please, sir, there's no ink." "Why is there no ink? The inkwells were filled yesterday," and so on. And just as the passengers on a ship soon do not hear the noise of the propeller, the pupils soon do not hear the teacher even when he wants them to listen. If there is any misbehavior while children are working silently, the teacher should check it by watching the child. If that does not stop it, he should walk quietly over to where the child is and, if necessary, scold him quietly. But if the teacher has any presence his look should be sufficient.

It is another fault of some young teachers that they do not cultivate good presence. Soldiers tend to despise an officer who neglects his appearance. His slovenliness is an insult to them, and he will not get good service from them.

A committee of experienced men or women appointing someone to take charge of others, often write off an interviewee from his appearance before he opens his mouth. The teacher should be an *important* person to his pupils if he is going to influence them for good, and he should dress, walk, talk, and conduct himself generally with dignity, quietness, and courtesy.

Many young teachers waste a great deal of time in getting children started on their work. Sometimes they are not in the room when the children arrive, the class becomes noisy, and time is lost steadying them down again. More time is lost at every change from class teaching to written work. Arguments with individual pupils should not take the teacher's attention off the class. Tell the children what they have to do, and say, "Anyone who can't begin, come out to the front." Pay no attention to those who have come out. Let them wait. Look at the class, and see that everyone is working. If necessary say, "Harris, have you not started yet?" and look at any other child who hasn't started. Of course, if it is only Harris who hasn't started, be silent and say nothing; he can be left while you attend to those in front. No pen, no ink, exercise book finished, and so on, are legitimate excuses which would delay the children starting to work, and so tend to form nuclei of noisy behavior. Unless there is already good discipline in the class, some such procedure is desirable. Free methods do not mean that children should waste half their school time in gossip and mischief.

If a teacher wants to hold the attention of his class his lessons must be interesting. This does not mean that he should decide what he wants to teach, and somehow or other stick interest on to it. I once had a student who had been a successful conjurer, and he had a very attractive manner. The children watched with intense interest when he began his lesson, but I left him while I visited another student in the school, returned in 10 minutes, and found, as I expected, that his class was out of hand. It is no use offering a cat nuts, even if they are attractively painted, nor expecting a squirrel to be interested in mice. If the subject matter itself is not interesting to junior school children, they should not be troubled with it. We have moved a long way from the view that it does not matter what a boy learns, so long as it is disagreeable enough. T. H. Huxley said, "Perhaps the most valuable result of all education is the ability to make yourself do the thing you have to do, when it ought to be done, whether you like it or not . . ."[60] This desirable end is easily achieved by free methods, if the free methods are properly used. We shall explain this later.

Meantime, let us not forget that classes can get out of hand and be very difficult to manage, and it is no justification for this state of affairs to say that one believes in free methods. It may be helpful to young teachers if I record how an experienced headmaster dealt with a very difficult class. Thirty boys aged 14-15 had been transferred to his school from temporary premises where they had been completely out of hand for weeks. They arrived at his school in the afternoon and were sent out for games where they behaved disgracefully, and two boys did not return to school after the games period.

The headmaster took the class himself next morning. He began in a friendly way, "Good morning, boys." "Good morning, sir." "Oh, by the way, before I begin, two boys did not return to school yesterday after games, John Smith and William Brown. John Smith, why did you not return to school?" "Please, sir, I was ill." "Oh, I'm sorry about that. Are you all right today?" "Yes, sir." "That's good."

"William Brown, what about you?" "Please, sir, I was

ill." "Dear, oh dear! Are you all right today?" "Yes, sir."
"Well I'm glad there was a good excuse, for I won't
allow any boy to play the fool in this school," and his
confident-looking eyes calmly covered every boy in the
class. "How many of you know your tables correctly up to
12 times? Is that all? Less than half of you! Well, now
you're in a good school like this you'll have to know all
your tables, not only up to 12 times, but 13 times, 14 times,
17 times, 19 times. How long do you think it will take you
to learn these? A year, you think? You think 18 months?
Well, I'm going to teach every boy in this class to do the
whole lot in 10 minutes, so pay attention," and he produced a large, simplified demonstration slide-rule, showed
the boys how it was used and how to make one for themselves, and gave them the necessary materials. The boys
were delighted and, with a little supervision from the
headmaster, gave no more trouble in the school.

Now note the clever psychology: the friendly approach;
the humorous handling of what everyone knew to be two
lies about illness; the clever assertion of his place as the
leader of the group, so that every boy feels in his unconscious mind, "I'd better be careful or this bold-looking
animal will kill me." The master does not overtly threaten
in any way. That would destroy the *unconscious* fear, and
on a conscious mind level they had little to fear from him.
But he does not depend on this unconscious fear. He
knows it won't last for long. Having dominated the class
by his good presence, and got them quiet and listening to
him, he plays for interest and a love relationship by beginning a well prepared lesson which he knows will make
an immediate appeal to the boys. It makes such a striking
appeal that these self-styled toughs are prepared to eat out
of his hand. This was a great leader whom they all admired
at once, and whom no young wolf thought for a moment

he could challenge successfully. Once the leadership of the class is definitely established, the good work can go on. Fortunately, not many classes are as difficult to handle, but all first-class teachers have this power in reserve so that they can cope with any difficulty which may arise. They take control of the situation by one strategem or another, whatever it is.

I was told how one of our East London headmasters once took charge of the situation at a church soiree. A great many children were sitting in the hall when the church workers came in with trays of cakes and sweets. There was some delay, and boys got out of their seats and began helping themselves from the trays. Others quickly followed, of course. The church workers lifted the trays above their heads, the children struggled to get up to the trays, and soon the hall was in pandemonium. The super-intendent asked this headmaster if he would help to restore order. The headmaster walked slowly up to the platform and looked at the mob as Moses might have looked at the Israelites when he saw them worshipping the golden calf. The noise decreased a little. When it was at its likely minimum, he gave one loud blast on his whistle. Another pause while the hall became quieter. Then in a loud, clear, voice, "Take all that food out!" The trays began to move away. The noise had stopped now, then slowly, "And it won't come back again till you are all in your seats!" The children all sat down quietly. One commanding look, one riveting sound, two short sentences, and order was restored. They had good class management, some of these old teachers.

Chapter Three

The Unconscious Mind

MANY PEOPLE BEFORE FREUD recognized the existence of the unconscious mind. Schiller, Schopenhauer, Nietzsche, Emerson, Eduard von Hartmann, Samuel Butler, and others had drawn attention to its importance. Illustrious scientists, artists, novelists, poets, and musicians have all told us how they made use of the unconscious mind in achieving their success, but for the most part we have ignored their remarks or attributed their creative achievements to a mysterious thing called "genius." Freud discovered the reality of the unconscious mind while working by the scientific method and he was delighted to find later how many important people had arrived intuitively at similar views. A great number of the classical references to the unconscious mind were discovered by Freud himself.

The unconscious mind functions in strange ways and it is not easy to understand at first the explanation that Freud or anyone else can give of it. It may be helpful as an introduction if we look at the problem in another way. Animals inherit instincts, that is to say they inherit not only the physical characteristics their ancestors acquired in order to adjust themselves to their environment, but they inherit tendencies to behave as their ancestors behaved. If a house dog does not get the chance of hunting with the pack as his ancestors did, *he will dream* he is hunting with the pack. His legs will make tentative running movements and he will give quiet little yelps as if he were joining in the hunt. Recent medical research shows that many animals, like human beings, dream for definite periods every night to help discharge these unused tendencies.[66] Human beings also inherit tendencies to behave as their ancestors behaved, and some of these tendencies are not suitable for the environment of a civilized community but they claim expression nevertheless. If they are repressed and denied expression, they will partly discharge themselves in dreams. Plato expressed it very well when he explained that the bad man does what the good man dreams. Now because most of these inherited tendencies were developed before speech, grammar, and logic were developed, dreams tend to express themselves in the more primitive form of visual images and symbolism, in a way which does not make sense to the conscious mind. When one wakens and recalls the dream, the conscious mind rearranges the details to try to make sense out of them, and often it does make sense but not the sense the dream intended. That is one of the reasons why dreams have puzzled mankind for ages, and why the interpretation of dreams is so complicated.

It was largely from his work as a neurologist, searching for the cause of neurotic illness in his patients, that Freud discovered the amazing richness of the unconscious mind and the theory of the interpretation of dreams. He found that the conscious mind is like the tip of the iceberg. The other seven-eighths of it, hidden out of sight, is like the unconscious mind. He found that neurotic illness was usually caused by people repressing innate tendencies to too great an extent, instead of steering them or sublimating them into acceptable behavior. Dreams cannot discharge all this bottled-up tension and it leaks out in a variety of strange ways. Lady Macbeth's sleepwalking and handwashing movements, for example, are familiar forms of neurotic behavior. Psychiatrists speak of the "washing mania." People tend to wash their hands to get rid of guilty thoughts. Pilate "took water and washed his hands before the multitude, saying I am innocent of the blood of this just person: see ye to it" (St. Matthew 27, 24.), and we have probably all heard people say, "I wash my hands of the whole affair."

Freud's findings have received confirmation in recent years from medical research workers studying sleep. Working in many different laboratories, they have arrived at the following remarkable conclusions: (a) We all dream every night for a total time of approximately ninety minutes, (b) The dreaming period is "physiologically so different from quiet sleep that many scientists began to refer to it as a third state of being—[a state that is] neither sleeping or waking. It resembled a lost continent of the mind,"[67] (c) If a subject is regularly wakened at the beginning of every dreaming period, he soon begins to show signs of neurosis. A control subject, wakened an equal number of times outside the dream period, is not affected. The dreaming periods are shown by electrical connections on the subject, and by rapid eye movements, checked at first, of course, by questioning the subject when he is wakened, and (d) Alcohol, barbiturates, tranquillizers, and amphetamines all reduce the dreaming periods, and have an adverse effect for this reason.[66]

Freud was a distinguished biologist, a doctor, and a specialist in neurology before he became a psychologist. He read Greek and Latin fluently, and spoke and wrote in German, French, and English. For six months he studied hundreds of cases of neurotic illness with Charcot at the Salpêtrière in Paris and went to study the surprising results Bernheim and others were obtaining with hypnosis. When he set up in practice as a specialist in neurology, he struggled for years trying to fit the strange symptoms of his patients on to his own rich background of neurology. But many of the symptoms were not related to neurology in any way and Freud, as a scientist, had to try to find new hypotheses which would hold these strange new facts. A woman might come to him, for example, because she had lost all feeling in her left hand. There was no doubt whatsoever that all feeling had been lost in the hand, but there is no nerve or set of nerves which supply the hand alone; the hand is not an anatomical unit. Freud found he could hypnotize the woman, tell her that when she wakened her hand would be normal again, and it was, perfectly normal. But she would return in a few days with a paralysis in the right arm, or severe headaches, or some other symptom, and so the trouble would be chased from one place to another. That was why Freud soon gave up hypnosis as a therapeutic procedure. Too often the results were transitory.

The many remarkable discoveries Freud made after he left neurology for psychology are published in 24 large volumes by the Hogarth Press. The easiest volume, and a good one to begin with, is *The Psychopathology of Everyday Life* (1901).[35] The first series of *Introductory Lectures* (1916-1917)[44] are also fairly simple, but one has to do a good deal of hard work before one can fully understand *The Interpretation of Dreams* (1901)[32] for example, a classic which has already been translated into almost every important language. We shall be referring later to some of Freud's discoveries.

Let us look now at a few of the statements great men

have given of their method of working. Poincaré, the mathematician said, "One is at once struck by the appearance of sudden illumination, obvious indications of a long period of unconscious work. The part played by this unconscious work in mathematical discovery seems to me indisputable."* Kekulé, after explaining how he discovered the chemical formula for benzene from dream images, said, "Let us learn to dream, gentlemen, then perhaps we shall find the truth . . . but let us beware of publishing our dreams before they have been put to the proof by the waking understanding."[61]

In *A Midsummer Night's Dream* we read,

The poet's eye, in a fine frenzy rolling,
Doth glance from heaven to earth, from earth to heaven;
And as imagination bodies forth
The forms of things unknown, the poet's pen
Turns them to shapes, and gives to airy nothing
A local habitation and a name.[76]

William Blake wrote,

"He who does not imagine in stronger and better lineaments, and in stronger and better light than his perishing mortal eye can see, does not imagine at all. The painter of this work asserts that all his imaginations appear to him infinitely more perfect and more minutely organised, than anything seen by his mortal eye. . . . I assert for myself that I do not behold the outward creation, and that to me it would be a hindrance, and not action. I question not my corporeal eye any more than I would question a window concerning a sight, I look through it, and not with it."[18]

Mozart in a letter to a friend says,

"What, you ask, is my method in writing and elaborating my large and lumbering things? I can in fact say nothing more about

* The remark was made at a lecture given to the Société de Psychologie in Paris, of which a good summary is given in *The Act of Creation* by Arthur Koestler.[65]

it than this; I do not myself know and can never find out. When I am in particularly good condition, perhaps riding in a carriage, or in a walk after a good meal and in a sleepless night, then the thoughts come to me in a rush, and best of all. *Whence and how— that I do not know and cannot learn* . . . all the finding and making only goes on in me as in a very vivid dream."[53]

We might consider in more detail how John Bunyan wrote *The Pilgrim's Progress*. Bunyan's father was a tinker, and John Bunyan followed his father's trade for a time. During the Civil War he served as a soldier, and after that he joined a society of Anabaptists and preached for them in public. Because of the severe laws against dissenters at that time he was put in prison, and kept there for 12 years. Released, he returned to his Anabaptist friends, began preaching again, and was put in prison again, this time for six months. It was during this second term of imprisonment that he wrote most of *The Pilgrim's Progress*. Now how did a man with that background write a masterpiece which has delighted cultured men and women for nearly three hundred years, and has been translated into more than a hundred different languages? Bunyan gives the answer in the Introduction he wrote to the book.

The Author's Apology for his Book

When at first I took my Pen in hand,
Thus for to write; I did not understand
That I at all should make a little Book
In such a mode: Nay, I had undertook
To make another; which was almost done,
Before I was aware, I this begun.
And thus it was: I writing of the Way
And Race of Saints in this our Gospel-day,
Fell suddenly into an Allegory
About their Journey, and the Way to Glory,
In more than twenty things, which I set down;

This done, I twenty more had in my crown,
And they again began to multiply,
Like sparks which from the coal do fly,
Nay then, thought I, if that you breed so fast,
I'll put you by yourselves, lest you at last
Should prove ad infinitum, and eat out
Thy Book that I already am about. . . .[5]

In other words, Bunyan let his unconscious mind take charge and write the book. Many writers do this. Edith Wharton wrote:

What I want to try to capture is an impression of the illusive movement when these people who haunt my brain actually begin to speak within me with their own voices. The situating of my tale, and its descriptive and narrative portions, I am conscious of conducting, though often unaware of how the story first came to me, pleading to be told; but as soon as the dialogue begins, I become merely a recording instrument, and my hand never hesitates because my mind has not to choose, but only to set down what these stupid or intelligent, lethargic or passionate, people say to each other in a language, and with arguments, that appear to be all their own.[84]

Now, as every child inherits the same kind of unconscious mind as these clever people do, why not let him use it? Emerson said, "There is a certain wisdom of humanity which is common to the greatest men with the lowest, and which our ordinary education often labors to silence and obstruct."[19] The child's essay which opens this book is obviously an unconscious mind production. He just let himself go and wrote without thinking too much. Darwin wrote in the same way. "Formerly I used to think about my sentences before writing them down; but for several years I have found that it saves time to scribble in a vile hand whole pages as quickly as I possibly can, contracting half the words; and then correct deliberately. Sentences thus scribbled down are often better ones than I could have written deliberately."[13]

The unconscious mind inherits the wisdom, knowledge, and skill of our ancestors, but it also inherits the tendency to behave as our Stone Age savage ancestors behaved. The purpose of education is to evoke from the unconscious mind the qualities which will be useful in a civilization, and to avoid arousing and evoking qualities which will not be useful. An intellect in tune with its unconscious is a much more powerful intellect, and our conscious mind decisions drawing on inherited knowledge, are much more reliable. Anatole France understood this when he wrote, "Reason, proud reason, is capricious and cruel. The sacred simplicity of instinct never betrays. In instinct dwells the sole truth, the only certitude that man may ever call his own in this life of illusion, where three-quarters of the ills from which we suffer come from our own thoughts," and, "My old friend Condillac says that the most intellectual people are precisely the most prone to fall into error."[28]

There is another aspect of the unconscious mind which is of importance for education. Freud found that we tend to repress into the unconscious, ideas which are unpleasant for us. Nietzsche had already referred to this:

'I did this,' says my Memory.
'I cannot have done this,' says my Pride,
and remains inexorable. In the end—
Memory yields.[72]

Freud saw that it was this unwillingness to face the truth which had made many of his patients ill. The repressed material did not lose its influence because it was apparently forgotten, but expressed itself in ways which caused serious confusion in some lives. Freud attached as much importance to the inherited unconscious as Jung did, but when it is a question of curing neurotic patients, the inherited unconscious is not so important as the more personal unconscious; the modifications the patient has made in his inherited "drives," and what has been repressed into the unconscious during his own lifetime.

As Freud was making most of his wonderful discoveries from what he found in treating patients, his published papers dealt very often with details which seemed in bad taste and frightened respectable people. But doctors and scientists must not avoid important evidence because it is unpleasant. It is not always unpleasant, however. Freud made a statement in one of his letters to Pfister (1928) which may surprise some people: "It really does happen that, in contrast to the usual state of affairs, the conscience, the better, the 'nobler' impulses suffer repression instead of the instinctually 'wicked' and unacceptable."[38]

I had a good example of this in an essay from a woman member of an extra mural class in psychology, which I was conducting: "My daughter was always telling me about a very wicked girl in the class. The children all disliked her, and the teacher disliked her. So I said to myself, 'Where is the good? It must be in the unconscious.' And I asked my daughter to try to get the girl to write out one of her dreams for me for an essay I was writing." The girl did, and the dream was enclosed for my information. This girl, who was unpleasant to everyone, was dreaming she was a nurse and looking after the old people and the sick people in the hospital, and was so happy doing good in her dream, because she could not make use of her good qualities in the everyday environment.

Now if someone did not help this girl, she might well have become a delinquent. And here I want to pay a tribute to all good teachers. Have they any idea how much the stability and good behavior in our nation is due to them? They gather up the instinctual interests of the children and sublimate them, thus giving the children new interests in life besides the primitive ones. But the brick building method of education does not help in this important work. There is no joy in such learning. Instinctive action is always pleasurable. Teachers who begin by repressing the unconscious minds of their pupils in order to build up walls of knowledge more effectively will not have much success. Let them look again at the thirty or forty living trees in front of them and see themselves trying to stick their bricks of knowledge on the living branches. What do children do with knowledge they don't want? They throw it off as soon as possible to keep their minds clear. Some will carry the bricks for a time to pass an examination, as children a generation ago carried them for a time to avoid the cane or the strap, but many present-day children can throw off such knowledge with a promptness and thoroughness which is surprising. And what are they left with? A large proportion of inherited "drives" at the primitive level, and a tendency to join the juvenile delinquents.

Of course many teachers maintain a living approach to their children even with what appears to be formal teaching. They always give interesting lessons with plenty of subject matter, and the children know they are loved. With rich subject matter, and the sunshine in the classroom, the roots are nourished and the tree can put forth new branches. Emerson, as usual, expresses the situation very well.

> The same reality pervades all teaching. The man may teach by doing, and not otherwise. If he can communicate himself he can teach, but not by words. He teaches who gives, and he learns who receives. There is no teaching until the pupil is brought into

the same state or principle in which you are; a transfusion takes place; he is you and you are he; then is a teaching, and by no unfriendly chance or bad company can he ever quite lose the benefit. But your propositions run out of one ear as they ran in at the other.[20]

Chapter Four

Early Education

Education in the Home

As the main traits of character tend to be fixed in the early years, we shall look first at the problem of education in the home. Man has evolved from the animals and carries in his physical structure vestiges of that heritage. Freud made the remarkable discovery that man also carries in his unconscious mind vestiges of all that his animal and savage ancestors thought and did. The baby in its development goes through the stages of evolution. It begins something like the amoeba, it develops branchial clefts which are similar to the developing gills of a fish, it develops further to a creature like a monkey, and is born as an immature human being more suited to move on all fours than to walk upright. And parents do not need Freud to tell them that some of the young child's behavior is very reminiscent of his animal and savage ancestors. Ontogeny repeats phylogeny in the mental sphere as well as in the physical.

On the other hand, young children can be very beautiful, mentally as well as physically. Some parents seem to have children with a preponderance of good qualities; other parents are not so lucky. The difference is largely a matter of how the children are handled; but the inheritance factor is also important, of course. The educational methods which were successful with one child may not be successful with the next one. Some children, by their inheritance, readily accept parental guidance, others are stronger willed and often resent interference. We can easily subdue the first type, but perhaps leave them without initiative, and we can easily evoke too much aggression in the second type, and make them unfit to mix with other people. A young child has not much control over his behavior. It takes time to build an ego structure. To this end, it is important that strong, primitive emotions should not be evoked from his unconscious for he cannot cope with them. Every thwarting of the child's instinctual behavior tends to generate and build up primitive aggression, either in his conscious or in his unconscious mind. As far as possible, therefore, the child should live in a simple environment where interference by the parent is not too often necessary. Similarly, primitive fear should not be evoked, or the foundation for the phobias may be built up for later life.

In the difficulties that inevitably arise the parent acts as a supporting ego for the child. Loud noises or quarrelling, for example, could cause panic, but if the parent appears unconcerned by the uproar the child will soon be reassured. I was at a picnic once with two parents and their children when the brushwood was accidentally set alight. While we men hurriedly moved some hen houses out of danger, the mother talked to the children as if this was a jolly good bonfire. No serious damage was done, and the children quite enjoyed the show. But another mother could have acted differently and left the children with exaggerated fears about fire. If a child is attracted to a flame or a hot stove, hold his arm and let him gradually feel the heat. He will soon draw his hand away. There is no need to let him burn himself to learn the danger.

Bad relations between parents, Freud tells us (1908), excite the emotional life of the child and "cause it to feel love and hate to an intense degree while it is still at a tender age,"[37] a view with which experienced people will readily agree. One of Freud's most astonishing discoveries was that the love interests of young children have a strong sexual background. In many ways they respond to love as adults do. They hate a rival, for example, and here they can show their primitive behavior, for if they were strong enough, they would kill him. In this connection, Freud (1916-1917) cited Diderot:

'Si le petit sauvage était abandonné à lui-même, qu'il conservât toute son imbécillité, et qu'il réunit au peu de raison de l'enfant au berceau la violence des passions de l'homme de trente ans, il torderait le col [cou] à son père et coucherait avec sa mère.'

('If the little savage were left to himself, preserving all his foolishness and adding to the small sense of a child in the cradle the violent passions of a man of thirty, he would strangle his father and lie with his mother.')[46]

As a rule, the infantile sexuality disappears from view about the age of five, and normal educational development proceeds steadily until puberty, when the sex interests reawaken. But if the infantile sexuality is considerably strengthened by experiences, the latency period, coming after five, may not develop and strong sexual interests may hinder normal education. Parents should be careful, therefore, that young children, even a two year old, should not see or hear parental intimacy. Some knowledge of adult sexual behavior is in the child's unconscious mind, and hints of it can evoke some of the excitement, jealousy, and aggression associated with that instinct, and disturb the young child's sleep and his serenity.

As far as possible, young children should be allowed to do what they want to do, so that they can gather up their inherited powers. They need *practice* in a great many inherited skills besides walking and talking in order to possess them, and they must do this in their own way. Freud quoted (1912-1913) what Goethe tells us in *Faust* (Part I, scene 1),

'Was du ererbt von deinen Vätern hast,
Erwirb es, um es zu besitzen.'

('What thou hast inherited from thy fathers,
acquire it to make it thine.')[40]

This does not mean, however, that children should rule the house, or make themselves a nuisance to other people. Parents should insist on obedience on important occasions. A child who has loving parents and gets plenty of outlet for his instinctual behavior is a contented child who welcomes guidance and accepts necessary discipline fairly easily. But a child who is continually thwarted develops undesirable degrees of stubbornness and aggression and almost automatically resists discipline of any kind.

The companionship of other children is very valuable. It would be a great educational advance if we could have nursery schools for all children, half time, perhaps, for the three year olds and then full time for a year or two before beginning the infants school. It is the early years that are most important. Raising the school leaving age can have nothing like the social value that good early training would have. Nursery school teachers know what to do, but for the sake of some mothers and others we may explain that the play in a good nursery school is of the greatest educational significance, not like the play with dozens of elaborate toys which one sees so often in modern homes, and which tends to weaken the child's powers of concentration. The most successful nursery school teachers teach as a good mother teaches—largely by intuition. Human mothers as well as animal mothers know instinctively a great deal about how to bring up their young ones. Unfortunately, many human mothers have had their mothering instinct spoiled by their own upbringing and find their children's behavior incomprehensible and maddening. They try, for example, to have their children toilet trained before two years of age, and by beginning too early often fail to achieve this by five or more. One of Freud's discoveries was that stubbornness in adult life is usually related to the toilet training in infancy. It was then that the more serious quarrels between mother and child began. Admonitions to say "Please" or "Thank you," and details of table etiquette should be left to a later age. It is a limited amount of interference any child can stand, and parents must sometimes interfere over more important things.

The fact that children identify themselves with their parents can produce some surprising results. A girl of 13 was not doing well in her grammar school and her father got her some private coaching in French. After a year she came bottom of the class in French and in most other subjects although she was an intelligent girl. The explanation was quite simple. Her mother was always boasting that she had been no good at school, meaning that she had not distinguished herself academically. The girl, who was always trying to keep in her mother's good books, was unconsciously trying to be "no good at school." This mother had apparently not encouraged independence sufficiently, and by exaggerating her own weakness in school had provided an unfortunate example.

Of course children, like trees and animals, can stand a lot of mishandling and survive; but parents who do not take good care of their children's education before five need not expect good results in schoolwork, or to see them in distinguished posts after school. The idea that there can be equality of opportunity in education by making all children of the same age-group go to the same school is a complete fallacy. Some have had a flying start by five and carry their ancestors' powers with them. Others have not only to start from scratch, but have to overcome all kinds of inhibitions which prevent them learning or concentrating on their work.

The strong impressions that early love, jealousy, and hate make on us is shown in some of our interests in literature. The young boy finds "Jack the Giant Killer" a good story. Generation after generation of adults find a curious fascination in the story of Oedipus, who killed his father and married his mother. Hamlet loved his father and hated his uncle who slept with his mother. Telemachus, in the *Odyssey,* loved his father and hated the suitors who wanted to sleep with his mother. This is the usual way in which the unconscious mind solves a love-hate relationship, namely by making two different persons out of the one. When the mother is divided into a Fairy Godmother, who provides all the good things (as happened early in life), and a wicked stepmother who ill-treats the little girl (won't let her have her own way in everything, as happened later), the little girl can easily identify herself with Cinderella, and enjoy the story. Many of the myths and fairy tales in all countries are derived from these early relationships with the parents.

Now let us see how a good school can carry on from these early years in the home. Another of the four schools to which the London teachers and headteachers were invited was the school for infants and juniors at Globe Road, Bethnal Green. The headmistress, Miss U. R. L. Greenwood, had also prepared a paper for the visitors, and with her kind permission I reproduce much of it here. From my point of view, the theory and practice are excellent.

"In this school we have never called our way of education by any particular name, we merely make our educational procedures as natural and sensible as we can. No school can be completely free, for all schools conform to some kind of system. What interests me is not that we call our system Activity Methods, or any other name, but that our system permits of natural and spontaneous movement and doing in education.

"Before discussing our methods, it will be helpful to know something about the underlying psychology upon which they are based. We realize that the child is not an empty being which the adult must fill by teaching. The child functions by his organs and by his instincts, he inherits the characteristics of his kind. He is not only a body but a spiritual embryo with latent psychic capacities which he will reveal, as little by little, he builds up his being. We therefore understand education in the sense of teaching and in the sense of this psychological development. We must help the child to develop his personality and we must adjust ourselves to him, rather than require him to adjust himself to us. We do not forget the power of the unconscious mind over human actions and we take as our goal the aid of its free functioning. The unconscious mind is like a creative aptitude by which the child builds up his mental world from the world around. It is an insatiable hunger that drives him toward his surroundings to find food for his spirit and nourishment for his growth, that leads him to a constant activity by which he endeavors to fulfill himself.

If he is denied free access to his total environment, if his spontaneous activity is repressed, he reacts and becomes naughty and restless. The conditions for a diminished level of functioning have been created. The living body and soul of a child grow through movement and activity; it is through movement and activity that the senses develop and the instincts function completely. From the mind's earliest development, with its need to possess and repeat pleasure, to do new things for the sake of doing them, activity is a fundamental urge. The joy of doing is the beginning of spiritual activity, it is a liveliness, an intensity of life.

"From these psychological facts we realize the supreme importance of movement in the child's development, and we can understand the reason for Activity Methods in education. They are methods based on natural law. That is, one cannot see the methods but one can see the child acting naturally and freely on the irresistable urge to contact things in his environment, and through his senses of sight and touch, assimilating knowledge. The child builds himself; the human personality forms itself, by itself. To understand the method one must watch the children. We see they learn in different ways—by their contact with each other—sometimes consciously copying another child—sometimes by absorbing the general atmosphere. They absorb much that is not actually taught but which they never forget. They learn by exploration, by constant repetition of the exercise, by creating. There is no single way of learning, all ways are right when they are based on the children's needs and the stage through which they are passing.

"Our first duty in Activity Methods, therefore, is to provide the right environment from which the child can build. (When there has been no preparation of suitable environment, the result is chaos and the children get no-

where.) Each classroom will have its own environment because each teacher will cater to the different periods of
growth and development through which the children pass.
The environment will be free of constraint, fear, and
punishment and the teacher will be sure that it contains
alluring materials to awaken concentrated attention. The
children must have a free choice of objects with which to
work and follow a sequence of actions to its completion.
This will give the inner contentment which comes from
achievement. Only when the work is completed will the
activity end; in order to make a bridge the child will have
to stick to his activity until the bridge is finished. *The
child is learning to persevere until a job is done.* For
Activity Methods to really succeed, the children must acquire this work attitude during their development.

"Through the medium of proper outer environment,
the children will create by continual activity, activity
which is real work. To the casual observer it will look
like play, but watch the children doing most seriously
what their mothers and fathers do—sweeping, dusting,
cooking, washing, heaving coal, building, cleaning windows—and it becomes clear they are not playing with toys,
they are fulfilling the vital instinct for work, and because
they love work they resent interruptions for trifles. When
the work is the result of an inner impulse it becomes a
fascinating and irresistible means through which the children develop intelligence, coordinate their movements,
acquire language and expression, and they must be allowed
to do it at their own speed.

Teachers are part of the children's environment and
we must adjust ourselves to the children's needs and
respect their personalities. In Activity Methods, teaching
facts is of minor importance. We realize that our major
business is to understand the unconscious processes of the

children's minds and we are aware that they will frequently understand facts much quicker by *doing* than by all our *talking*. We shall need great patience to try to know when not to give useless assistance; often our help means the children stop work, they no longer act for themselves, it is we who are acting through them. But we also realize the children need guidance and training and it is our job to know when to give them. In the midst of the children's activities they will yet need succor and security; they need a substitute for mother and father to whom they can come for help, and the teacher must assume this role. But to be forty mothers and fathers at once is not possible; we can only have that relationship with each child individually, and the individual Activity Methods make this relationship more possible.

"In arranging the environment it is advantageous, where possible, to rearrange the classroom. I always think it is good to break away from the formal appearance of the rows of desks; they look so stiff, so horribly uninteresting and depressing, and I feel this depression makes a child unconsciously dislike school and learning. To me, they are soul destroying and I believe some children must find their stiff immobility frightening. Where there is stepping, or the rooms are small, rearrangement is usually impossible, but where it can be done, it makes for a far happier atmosphere.

"Upon these principles we try to fashion our activities. It would be difficult to describe to you exactly the method in our school. I, personally, act largely by intuition and instinct. I might plan a lesson most carefully, but when I am in the classroom with the children, the time will be spent in an entirely different way, and I am sure the children will have learned more than if I had kept to my plans! Each teacher is a different personality and while keeping in mind fundamental principles, will interpret things differently. Just as the children are free to develop, the teachers are also free to experiment and to construct their environment.

"This raises the much debated idea of freedom, which has so many interpretations. It may appear at a first visit that our behavior in this school is quite unbridled; the children come and go without constraint, they are not marshalled along in lines, they are not strictly supervised on the stairs, or in the corridors, or cloakrooms, they skip or run or walk as they feel, though when in a crowd we do insist they walk. They laugh and talk and have fun on the way; the six and seven year olds particularly love a friendly wrestle and roll-over along the hall as they go to their rooms. There are not a multitude of petty rules and regulations which they must remember, and there is always free, spontaneous, and happy conversation with the teachers. But this does not mean they are *always* running about, or that they are always doing just as they wish—it does not mean that they can always make a noise. They must regard other people's feelings, they must consider the safety of others, they must remember the code of good manners which is based on consideration for others, they must remember the necessary fundamental rules of law and order; there are times when silence and stillness are essential. To us, freedom means the children should have opportunities to learn self-control, opportunities to realize that to be free means control from within, opportunities and scope to develop all their functions. Above all, I feel it should be the opportunity for their growing progressively independent of adults. They should gain control over their movements, they should be able to concentrate on work in which they are absorbed and interested, and I am sure Activity Methods are a means of attaining all

[58]

of this. An unconscious discipline of movement grows through activity; it is not extraneous discipline, it comes from within, which is the source of true freedom. To this end the teacher must provide an environment in which children can work and play, discover, invent, and create; one in which the social and cooperative instincts develop, in which the children are happy, and when they are happy they will be good.

Nursery Class

"In this school the first period of development we have to deal with is the nursery class age; the stage when children are highly individual and absorbed in their own affairs. It is a period of spontaneous exploration. They have their workrooms and playrooms, their sleeping room, their dining room, and their playground, with space to move freely at their own time and in their own way. Here we provide opportunities for them to choose their own occupations and to experiment with materials. These children are four and five years old, the age when the sheer appetite for movement must be satisfied. It is the age when the instinctive desire to touch and discover, to learn unconsciously by constant repetition of movement, must be gratified. There is the urge to act impulsively in choosing and carrying out their activities. The teacher has to consider all these needs when preparing the environment for the nursery class.

"At this age they feel the desire to act as they have seen others act. It is not immediate imitation but something observed which has been stored away. Children love to perform actions performed by adults; it is one of the vital relations between adult and child. Many of their activities, therefore, are associated with domestic or social surroundings. The children love brooms and pans, pails and mops; they sweep, dust, wash up, polish, wash clothes and hang them out to dry. They are mothers and fathers, they have their playhouses containing the necessary objects for these activities: the dresser, cups and saucers, plates, jugs, tables and chairs. They send their children shopping, they go to visit relatives by train and bus, which they construct from chairs and upturned tables. The children use all sorts of apparatus—boxes, wood, spoons, pots and pans, pieces of material, sieves for sand, kettles and old teapots with spouts for pouring water, rubber tubing, funnels—and these are much better than expensive toys.

"Damp sand is an invaluable material for building and for use with spades and buckets, wooden spoons, and boxes. The children use it in a large sand trolly round which four to six can play at once. Dry sand in an old bath is another delight; this they can run through their fingers and through sieves and funnels.

"Water is a constant source of fun and, like sand, it is a delight in itself. Only supply a zinc trough, old baths, basins, jugs and teapots to fill, floating toys, shells, corks, rubber tubing, and stones, and the children have endless pleasure and experiences. Mixing water with sand and clay and gaining the idea of thinning substances is always absorbing. Water is a primitive plaything, from splashing and feeling to pouring and filling, it leads to further water interests; interest in taps, drainpipes, cisterns, the fireman's hose, and, if the child is lucky enough to have freedom to explore, the foundation for understanding hydraulics is unconsciously absorbed.

"Clay is another essential material; children love to rub it through their fingers just for the instinctive pleasure of it. They take it from the clay bin in large lumps, and there is spontaneous laughter and joy when they are thumping and banging it down. At this age the children are not so much concerned about making things with clay as with this instinctive urge to have their hands full of it, to twist and to roll and to pound. Later on they make their rolls and cakes and animals and whatever interests them. I have often noticed that playing with clay and water is most satisfying for nervous children; it seems to free their energy which otherwise remains unsatisfied. Children can control clay and sand and water and their unconscious sense of power is gratified.

"Work with bricks is perhaps equally important. Bricks introduce an element of difficulty and give the children a sense of greater control. We try to obtain bricks of all sizes, shapes, and colors; those nearly the size of real building bricks, all-purpose inch cube bricks (the most useful of all), and hollow cardboard bricks (the least durable of all). Boxes of every size do nicely as bricks. With the bricks or their substitutes, the children use pieces of wood of all lengths and sizes for their construction activities, which usually take place on the floor.

"Children are fond of wheeled toys and one of their favorites is an old wooden sugar box on strong wheels; they can get into it and be wheeled about, it is a bus, a lorry, or whatever they decide. They are no longer content to pull and push their wheeled toys—they want to use them for a definite purpose—to ride in them, to use them for transport, to load them with bricks and other materials —they want to put them to practical use.

"Other outstanding toys that give great satisfaction are the slide, the seesaw, large engines and motor cars which they can drive, scooters, dolls' prams with dolls, soft animals, and of course, balls: footballs, wool balls, small wooden balls, even medicine balls. These are all of different weights and give different bumps and sounds and unconsciously much is learned about the density of material. The children also love toys which make a noise. A percussion band fills this need and sticks and empty tins make many of the instruments. Drawing and painting are further delights. They use large brushes and large sheets of paper (any paper we can get, backs of posters, newspapers, large wrapping paper) with charcoal for the drawing. At first the children will splash about in a purely exploratory way, but as time goes on skill increases to deliberate shaping, and the stage of creation is reached.

"Thus at this early stage the little ones are learning unconsciously through getting the feel of things, exploring, developing creative skill. They are happy in the freedom which allows for the functioning of the unconscious mind and for the development of their personalities.

Infants School

"We now pass on to the infants school, when the children are eager and ready to enter the bigger world and use it as their servant for their developing imaginations. They are more able to control their bodies and objects in their environment, they are more fluent in speech and in the interchange of ideas, but they are still small and they want to be big like the grown-ups around them. They are seeking for new power and they enter into imaginary relationships as a form of compensation for their littleness. Imagination directs their work and play.

"The environment for these children is full of materials very similar to those in the nursery classes, but they are used in different ways and for different purposes. The children's treatment of the various materials is more specialized, and the unplanned attack of the younger child is gradually replaced by a more carefully planned application of skill. Objects made with clay and sand are becoming quite cleverly constructed for use in their imaginative play. Water plays an important part in their activities, as it did in the nursery classes, but now they are the captains of the boats they sail, they are the milkmen when they fill their bottles—unconsciously getting measurement values—discovering for themselves that water will find its own level.

"Dolls are perhaps more important at this stage than before, and each class has whatever dolls we can collect. Dolls can be put to bed—they do as they are told—they can be bathed and undressed—they do not answer back, they give unconscious and conscious power to these little children. Each classroom should have a property box containing old lace and net curtains for cloaks, and crowns and swords so that the children can become kings and queens enjoying new experiences in movement and perhaps in speech, reaching out in new directions and gaining in power of expression. Fairy stories are real to these children. They have an insatiable hunger for them and to act them is their crowning delight.

"Realistic toys are not so necessary at this stage; they are not so interesting or useful in imaginative activities as improvised toys. I watched a small boy of six rig up a horse from an old form and an upturned chair; to him the horse was galloping and his job was to jump on and off its back while it continued to gallop. In one room the children love using old drawing models which are large, hollow, white wooden cubes and hexagons. They serve as towers, castles, thrones, cargo in ships, material for transport in lorries, and as luggage in their porter's barrow. I have noticed that specialized number apparatus is often used for making trains and ships, but at the same time, the children are unconsciously assimilating number values.

"The children revel in pretending to read. We print

nursery rhymes and little stories and sentences under pictures which we hang about the room, and they enjoy going from picture to picture, reading the words underneath and becoming familiar with the different shapes of the letters and look of the words. Later we hang pictures with single words underneath. We make separate large cards on which the same words are printed and these are used for matching. The children take a card from its box and place it underneath the word on the picture, they compare them, bring the card to read to the teacher, and write the word in their books or on their millboards. Later they match letters and learn the sounds these symbols make. In this fashion we begin to combine the sentence and phonetic methods of reading in an active way. The children progress to simple books, then to harder sentences, and on to harder books. This leads to writing simple diaries and original stories and to writing and posting letters, which is an exciting activity. From their imaginary scribbles, to the words and sentences they have been matching and reading, to the time when they begin to write freely in their own way about things which interest them, writing is consistently combined with reading.

"The poems and songs which the children learn are also printed in large print or script and hung in the classroom. I have often watched a lone child in his free time, singing his songs and following the words on the song sheets. Juniors like to do this just as much as infants.

"During this age of imagination, and in fact throughout the infants and junior school, most children like to have a special corner of their own for reading. They escape from their chair or desk to some cubbyhole which in their fantasy becomes a cave, a wigwam, their backwoods hut, or their cosy dream home. Somehow, in this way, reading becomes much more interesting than when confined to a desk. It is not necessary to sit at a desk in order to read or even to write. In one room we have a large square table under which a group of children love to read and carry on their activities, and they alone know in what faraway world they are living. Large strong packing cases turned up on end are other favorite hideouts. One teacher arranged her low cupboards to make a small enclosed space where the children loved to work rather than at their desks.

"You will realize all these activities must also involve a great deal of teacher direction, and it is the wise teacher who will use the interests of the children in teaching them reading, writing, and arithmetic and the other subjects of the curriculum. Teachers will provide the material in the environment to stimulate interest, they will use this material in their class talks and demonstrations. A general shop with scales and weights, for example, is part of the environment. The shop usually consists of dummy articles: fruits and cakes made from clay, boxes of acorns, chestnuts, pine cones, beechnuts, sand, sawdust, shell, corks, bottle tops, and small stones; all things which can be easily weighed. In their imaginative play the children call many of these by other names; they become biscuits, sweets, sugar, and so on. But at some time the teacher has explained the pound weight, the ounce, four ounces, eight ounces, and in their play they will weigh material over and over again, learning these measures consciously and unconsciously; pounds and ounces are real to them, not abstractions. The teacher has written the table of weights, which will hang near the shop, to which the children can refer. In a class talk, the teacher will also show them the names they want for their stock-in-trade and a list will be made to hang near the shop from which the children can copy the names to be put on their labels and bills. These shops are not elaborate constructions; the best shops are just long tables which provide plenty of room and allow for free movement. The children use liquid measures in the same way, experiencing for themselves pints and quarts and gallons. Here too, they can refer to a table of measures which they have talked about with the teacher and which hangs in the room.

"They use money with these activities, cardboard money usually, but sometimes they make coins and occasionally the children use real money. This leads to talks about money and writing down the symbols, to making bills, and eventually to money sums in the more directed class work. Skittles is a favorite game, and writing the scores for each side, as well as finding the totals, are other real pieces of arithmetic. The children learn their tables by means of inch cube bricks or other small bricks, and by table boards. Table boards are pieces of plywood, strung with beads in rows, something like the ancient abacus. The table boards are in rows of two beads, others are in rows of three beads, others in four, and so on; these can be used whenever the children need them. At the same time the mathematical tables are written by the teacher and hung in the classroom for the children to refer to and learn as they need.

"All mathematical calculations are taught by material in the environment of the classroom. Cube bricks are the most satisfactory material—they are comfortably handled and easy to place—all the fundamental calculations can be discovered—and there is unconscious stimulation of the very sense of mathematics in the actual handling of these bricks. I have a piece of apparatus based on the cube brick, by which the values and processes can be experienced and calculation simplified. Little children can use it individually and discover much by themselves, while junior children, and even seniors, find it a great help. It consists of bars made of 10 cube bricks and the one hundred block made with 10 bars or one hundred cube bricks. You will have realized it has tremendous possibilities. [See Figure 1, p. 97.]

"While activities go on the teachers are busy helping groups of children and individual children. They keep progress records, watch the activities and take part in them, discover the children's different abilities, characteristics, and creative aptitudes, watch to see where help and guidance are needed, and are ready with advice, suggestions, and sympathy. With large classes it is necessary to gather the children together for class talks—to demonstrate a new discovery or rule—to introduce new words and new kinds of spelling—to discuss the news sheet or weather report— to become acquainted with special poems or songs —to point out and enforce habits of tidiness and order— to write diaries—for the story period. Teachers must economize in effort when possible. Working arrangements may often require silence as being best for all, but inevitably discussions will arise and along with them, noise. When children are absorbed in their work and when there is a real sense of purpose this noise is not disturbing.

Junior School

"From the infant stage of fantasy and imagination we pass to the junior stage, when children put their imaginations into real experiences. They want real warfare when gangs fight each other. They are at the very height of their physical strength and vitality; they are conscious of their own strength. It is the time of greatest mental and physical activity; the noisy period when children want to prove their power over material things. They are at the practical age, the age of reality. The group

[67]

begins to play a dominant part in children's lives, they require to work and play in a group where they can show off and have an audience. These children always organize into small groups, never into a crowd. If you watch them in their free play they organize themselves naturally into small groups of three or four, perhaps six, even eight, but never more. In these groups their social qualities are realized, which is a necessary condition for their growth. Even in art, groups of children will often work together and the mystery is that all their drawings fit together so marvellously well. I have been into a classroom to speak to the teachers, and while talking have watched these groups drawing rapidly and surely, fitting in each drawing without hesitation, and quite unconscious that I was watching. It is the same in clay modelling and other handicrafts; the children like to make their individual model to add to a combined piece of work.

"When we consider the characteristics of the junior stage, we understand that Activity Methods are equally as important for these children as for the infants and the nursery children. The rooms should resemble practical workrooms where the subjects of the curriculum can be worked out in movement. There should also be a corner for a library and places for quiet work. How wrong are the small classrooms packed with desks, and little room to move about! It makes it so much more difficult to carry out Activity Methods with juniors than with smaller and younger children. We in this school have been fortunate, for in recent years, since 1946, we have not been faced with this particular difficulty. We have created space by making two small classrooms into one, and the juniors can move about as freely as the little children. Of course, as they grow older they are able to concentrate for longer periods and they spend more time sitting down because more of the jobs they wish to do are sedentary.

"The familiar materials used in the infants school are seen in the junior classes—paints, large paper, sand, clay, water, bricks, liquid measures—the shop with scales and weights and materials for weighing—jigsaw puzzles—dominoes—pegboards—the carpenter's table—tools and wood—the old telephone. More difficult and complicated games, like chess, are included for the 10 and 11 year olds, while at the same time, dolls and their accessories and the place for a home continue to be important. But the materials in the environment are used with a difference. The nursery children and the infants use activity and materials to free their souls—it is a period of functioning—a means of developing—it helps in their games of fantasy and imagination. Juniors use materials, and activity more especially, as a mean to an end. The materials they use in each activity help them to become more effective and skilled, more capable of abstract and critical thinking; infants use cube bricks mostly for imaginative play—to build towers and castles—juniors use them for finding the square and the cube of eight. Juniors will weigh sand and sawdust, cones and acorns, and compare the density of materials. Infants use paint and brushes and crayons just for the joy of painting and creating a picture quickly. Juniors are much more absorbed in the choice of color, in the mixing of color, in the technical makeup of the picture. The freeing of the dream mind—the unconscious mind—is more apparent. They also enjoy a purpose for their art such as making covers for their individual work. Infants and juniors read for the joy of reading and enjoying a simple tale, but juniors can use their reading for research as well. The junior is active in directing his thinking toward the solution of problems.

[69]

"The group instinct in the junior school is a help in dramatic work. They relish making up their plays and working together to attain the finished production. In our second class they are working at the scenery and effects for their own nativity play for Christmas. Through group work, the top junior boys made toys for every nursery class child for Christmas. This was a big undertaking for the toys were large and strong and worked; they were made mostly from scrap material and were gaily painted in bright colors, and the little ones were delighted.

"And what are the children's reactions to activities rather than mass class teaching? They become absorbed in concentrating on the work in hand and are oblivious to external stimulus. I often go into rooms when they are so engrossed and busy that they do not notice me. I have taken visitors into classrooms, but the children remained unaware of these strangers. Not long ago, a very tall, very dark, and altogether strikingly handsome man from Java visited us. As we prepared to visit the classrooms he told me he was used to being stared at. How amazed he was when the children did not notice him until he spoke to them individually. Their surprise was only momentary, they were soon concentrating again on the activity they had in hand. This impressed him more than the children's work.

"Another feature of Activity Methods is that children will repeat an exercise over and over again. Infants and juniors do this, thus unconsciously fixing certain facts in their minds. I remember the teacher of the top class of juniors telling me she had not taught them weights and measures, but they all knew how to do these sums through constantly experimenting with scales and measures. By means of a fixed rule on the wall children will measure themselves and their friends over and over again. It is quite thrilling to measure their feet and their shoes and the length of their frocks, and to make comparisons. Children will creep back into their rooms if they get the chance, during play or in the dinner hour, in order to play with their shops and other materials. The value of the activity lies in the spontaneous desire to use it, and to play with it, until the desire is exhausted and the knowledge to be gained has been assimilated—then it is time to go on to something else.

"And for the teachers? They need to understand the children's periods of growth, to constantly plan and arrange the environment. Large classes make it hard and tiring work—do not undertake it if you want an easy time. Above all, you need an innate sympathy and love for children and a willingness to be guided by them—realizing that of such is the Kingdom of Heaven."

Now although the two schools described were in old buildings,* the children from one of the poorest parts of London, and the classes each of forty pupils, any modern educationist would say that these children were being educated in a remarkably efficient way; so much so that he would find it difficult to suggest any improvement in the educational procedure. The children all felt free and happy, the discipline was excellent and the standard of work was much higher than it was in the more formal schools. Visiting headteachers were very much impressed.

One might think that in these happy schools it would be easy to continue with work of this kind. When a teacher was promoted to a headship or retired, her place could be taken by a young teacher from the training college, and as she would be trained in modern methods, all would be well. But this is not what happens. It is more likely

* Mrs. Howlett's school was built in 1873, Miss Greenwood's school in 1874.

that the young teacher would soon have a class of rather noisy children learning very little. It must not be forgotten that these well-behaved and happy children have in their unconscious minds tendencies to behave as their savage ancestors behaved, and while these tendencies will lie dormant if we leave them alone, they can flare up if evoked. It is difficult enough for a man to love two women at once, and it is not any easier to love forty children at once without arousing jealousy and aggression. Much the easiest form of teaching is formal teaching with a tidy class and graded textbooks, and even this is difficult enough for a teacher straight from college. All the successful Heads I know who have free schools, ask most young teachers to carry on with formal methods for a time until they have acquired good class control and have many successful lessons at their command. They can then begin free methods, a little at a time, and they can return to the tidy class and formal methods if things become too difficult. Quite a lot of technical skill is required to control forty children who are free to do what they want to do.

It is one of the difficulties of running a first-class school on free methods that teachers who are successful at this work tend to be appointed to headships. An infants and junior school near Miss Greenwood's school was running on similar free methods until five of the best teachers left for headships in one year. Their places were taken by five young women just out of college. The headmistress wisely changed over to more formal methods in these five classes and did not allow free methods elsewhere to interfere with this formal work. As the young teachers got more experience and more skill, she *gradually* introduced free methods again, and soon had as good a school as before. But it took more than a year to get back to free methods in all classes. While classes are large, all teachers must be able to use the more formal methods in order to survive. Activity Methods put a greater strain on the teacher, and he is not always in good health and spirits. If he cannot train his class to sit at their desks and be quietly employed for a time, the teacher and the children will not get the periods of peace and quietness which they all need.

A more serious situation arises when a successful Head has to retire, and a new Head is appointed who does not understand the importance of the unconscious mind. He sees the lack of sequence in the teaching and this and the apparent lack of discipline disturb him. He tends to tidy the place up a little, gradually asserts his authority a little more, and, of course, soon prevents the unconscious minds of the children from functioning appropriately. Some of the teachers who like to work by free methods find they cannot use free methods in that atmosphere and transfer to other schools. Soon the headmaster has a "well-disciplined" school, with good sequence in all the teaching, and nice tidy books all carefully corrected in red ink. Some people with no knowledge of the importance of the unconscious mind may even think he has improved the school. There is a place for good sequence in certain lessons, but many teachers make too much of it. A headmaster knows a lot about education, but he did not learn it in sequence. From his conversation, reading, and experience he collected the details which interested him and ignored the others.

One of the good teachers in my district told me he had had an interview for a headship and was one of three for the final interview. "What questions did they ask you?" I inquired.

"The chairman asked if I had done anything to insure a good sequence of work with the junior school. I told him that I was responsible for the geography teaching and I had gone to the two junior schools which fed our senior school, and arranged syllabuses of work with the teachers who taught geography there, so that there was perfect sequence in the teaching. The committee," he added, "seemed very pleased."

"As man to man, Mr. A," I said, "tell me this, do the children from the junior schools know *any* geography when they come to you?"

"No, sir," he replied.

Chapter Five

Secondary Education

WHEN THE ALL-AGE schools were divided into junior and senior schools, soon after 1930, the results were not what people had anticipated. Syllabuses had been prepared by education experts to give the seniors a good academic education, but it was soon found the children were not ready for work of this kind. It had been assumed if children spent say, 120 hours learning geography in the junior school, they would all know some; but it was surprising how many children knew no geography at all. The same lack applied to history and mathematics; teachers were disappointed to find that some seniors did not even know the multiplication tables. In the all-age school the children had been promoted partly by age, but largely by attainment, so the top class was composed of intelligent and well-informed children. It looked as if this was the result of good teaching in all the lower classes. The children were the brightest in the school, but the age range in the top class was usually considerable. There were probably some 14-year-olds doing reasonably well among the 12-year-olds, some 12-year-olds among the 10-year-olds, and some eight-year-olds learning to read among the six- and seven-year-olds. When some of the brightest pupils went off to Grammar and Technical Schools, and all the remaining pupils of 11 plus were transferred to the new senior schools, they included some very backward children.*

I inspected numbers of these senior schools after they had been going for five or six years, and again the results were surprising. Many of the schools, especially in the poorer areas, were doing valuable social work, but the pupils ready to leave showed a dismaying absence of academic knowledge. The teaching and class examinations appeared to be satisfactory, but it seemed that the pupils could forget information just about as quickly as teachers could put it in. Some pupils would remember it for a time to please the teacher or to gain marks for their House, but then they were free to forget all about it. Many teachers told me the children seemed to have no ability to retain knowledge; but of course university professors and successful businessmen have no ability to retain knowledge either if they don't want it.

It has been said that "Education is what remains when we have forgotten all we have ever learned," but the learning and forgetting which I found is not what is meant by the remark. It means that a games player is never good until he can forget the details of his techniques, or, in the larger sense, that knowledge which has matured into wisdom is valuable. In other words, knowledge is sometimes most valuable when it has become unconscious knowledge. Administrators and barristers do a good deal of learning

* Grammar Schools prepare the brightest pupils for the universities. Technical Schools accept suitable pupils, but the standard for admission is not quite so high as it is for the Grammar Schools. The remainder of the pupils, eighty or ninety per cent of them, went to the ordinary senior school. After 1944, the senior schools were called Secondary Modern Schools. Admission to Grammar and Technical Schools was by an examination at the age of 11 plus, modified to some extent by the report of the Head of the junior school. The Comprehensive School educates children of various abilities in one large building, so that an examination at 11 plus is not necessary.

and forgetting and are well paid for it, but it is difficult to see what advantage the pupils had gained from the procedure. The authorities began to realize that if there was no obvious penalty for not knowing what had been taught, the children would behave like adults and ignore all information they did not want.

After the 1944 Education Act, a real effort was made to improve the senior schools in order to give them parity of esteem with the Grammar Schools. Buildings, staffing, libraries, science laboratories, rooms equipped for woodwork, metalwork, domestic science and so on were all provided on the same scale as the Grammar Schools. The senior schools became Secondary Modern Schools, and some were even better equipped than the neighboring Grammar Schools. It was difficult, however, to get well-qualified teachers for science, mathematics, and other subjects, and when occasionally a specialist teacher was appointed, he again found the children were not ready for advanced work. Now that we know more about the unconscious mind and the great importance of the early years, we are less inclined to attribute this backwardness to a low intelligence quotient or other innate weakness. Inheritance counts for a lot in education, but more people now realize that children whose education has been neglected in the home, or in the early years at school, cannot compare at 11 years of age with children whose early interests have been encouraged and fed by their parents, and who have gone to infants and junior schools of the excellent types described in the preceding chapters. We cannot give equality in education if we only begin at 11 years of age.

Observers had the strong feeling that the Secondary Modern School, with all its new amenities, had not the prestige of the Grammar School, and there was evidence that the 11 plus examination excluded from Grammar

School education many pupils who would have profited from it. The idea of the Comprehensive School now became popular with education authorities and many parents. All children of 11 plus would go to the same school which would provide a variety of courses, and then pupils would not be separated at 11 plus into what looked like superior and inferior groups. It should be easier too, to move a child who was a late developer into a more academic class. The first few Comprehensive Schools built in London seemed to be very successful and the Labor government which was in office until June 1970 was trying to make this form of secondary education compulsory for all local education authorities. But many educationists are not happy about the *haste* in making this important change. They point out that if a fine new school is built and twice the average salary offered to the new Head, a good Head will be appointed; if large Special Allowances are offered, a good staff will be obtained. This means a good school on any plan; but we cannot go on taking the best of the local education staff in this way. It is also pointed out that it will take many years to build the new large schools, and that to call two old buildings a mile apart a Comprehensive School under one Head, and to break up a good Grammar School in order to get Grammar School pupils for the Comprehensive School, is not necessarily an educational advance and might well be an educational setback.

There are advantages and disadvantages in the Comprehensive scheme of education, and it would be better, some think, to introduce the plan gradually to see how these balance out. We should not assume that all trained teachers are good teachers who can do without the personal guidance and support of the headmaster. When a school has a roll of over five hundred pupils the Head loses much of his personal control of the staff and it is not easy to delegate this control. There may also be a tendency in schools of two thousand pupils to make the teaching more formal. This does not happen in Eton and Harrow, of course, but classes there are much smaller and teachers more highly paid and better qualified. The Comprehensive School does not eliminate the problem of learning and forgetting, needless to say, and thought must still be given to the question of feeding the true interests of the pupils, as was so successfully done in the junior schools we have described.

Many years ago, a master at Harrow School was so remarkably successful in teaching physics that the Board of Education, as it then was, arranged for physics masters in Grammar Schools to spend some time at Harrow to study his very successful technique. Some of the visitors were disappointed. They asked for a copy of his syllabus. He had no syllabus. They tried to elicit his procedure. Would he teach this before that? "Yes, if the boy wanted it." "But surely you would not teach B before A?" "Oh yes, if the boy wanted that." As one of the visitors said jokingly, "That infernal 'boy' seems to upset everything." Of course it was the fact that the master followed the interests of each boy, and not a syllabus, that made his work so successful. The boy was then making his scientific knowledge an extension of his instinctual interests, and thus part of himself. All instinctive action is pleasurable, and the boy would not forget the knowledge he had acquired. This is the way the real scientist works. "All great discoveries," Sir William Bragg once said, if I remember rightly, "were made by men who worked for the fun of it."

Students with good memories can remember a mass of scientific details presented in logical sequence, and some can even acquire good Honors Degrees on the knowledge.

[79]

But experienced scientists making scientific appointments are not taken in by memorized scientific knowledge, and such students find themselves at a disadvantage at interviews, or when they have to do scientific work on their own. The master at Harrow had small classes and several laboratories, and that made a difference; but one of the Grammar School masters arranged a large number of experiments, wrote cards explaining each, and as far as he could, allowed each pair of pupils to choose what experiment they wanted to work at. The procedure was very successful and he retained it.

Einstein was very critical of the usual method of teaching science. He wrote:

> I soon learned to scent out that which was able to lead to fundamentals and to turn aside from everything else, from the multitude of things which clutter up the mind and divert it from the essential. The hitch in this was, of course, the fact that one had to cram all this stuff into one's mind for the examinations, whether one liked it or not. This coercion had such a deterring effect [upon me] that, after I had passed the final examination, I found the consideration of any scientific problems distasteful to me for an entire year. . . . It is, in fact, nothing short of a miracle that the modern methods of instruction have not yet entirely strangled the holy curiousity of inquiry; for this delicate little plant, aside from stimulation, stands mainly in need of freedom; without this it goes to wreck and ruin without fail.[17]

I would like students to begin scientific studies in laboratories equipped with simple and safe apparatus with which they could be trusted. Pupils who know no science cannot be allowed freedom to experiment in a laboratory where there are strong acids and poisonous salts, or expensive and delicate equipment. They could well begin as some East London boys began in an elementary school more than forty years ago, with a master who was interested in science. I quote from his letter:

[80]

The boys came to me in sections of 24, worked in pairs, passing from one experiment to another, making their own observations and recording them in loose-leaf notebooks, which they kept throughout the course.

Some of the experiments were: (a) Running colored water through a burette to find the capacity of beakers, cups, and bottles, (b) Measuring up galvanized tanks and cisterns borrowed from a local works, and calculating the volume, (c) Burning substances [such as] lead in open and closed crucibles, (d) Graduating thermometers, (e) Making simple electrical models, electric magnets, induction coils, and (f) Simple analysis—heating potassium chlorate in a test tube and plunging in a glowing splint.

They could weigh and measure in the metric system (I had six balances), manipulate the screw gauge and spherometer, and they had a fair knowledge of specific gravity.

Any master with scientific knowledge could soon arrange other elementary experiments for the pupils. They could work pulleys, make explosions with little tins of gas and air, crush tins with atmospheric pressure, blow glass bulbs, learn about latent heat, reflection and refraction of light, and lines of force. They could play with the sinews of a hen's foot and leg and be introduced to the marvels of the human hand. The master could show the closing of the fingers by the muscles of the forearm pulling on sinews, explain how little "loops" at each joint keep the sinews from interfering with the grip and talk about the oil glands for lubricating these "loops." He might ask why the hand is not pulled over along with the fingers, leading to exploration of the sinews on the back of the hand and the antagonist muscles, and then to the "automatic telephones" between the prime movers and the antagonist muscles. A good anatomical diagram would show more of the miracles, and the children would have another bit of science to wonder about.

Chapter Six

School Subjects

It is easier to explain the importance of the unconscious mind to a university extension class of older men and women, than it is to explain it to a class of university students who have just taken their degrees. The students, from their background of study, tend to take a logical, intellectual view of problems and they find it difficult to accept the fact that the unconscious mind has not learned logic, and does not even trouble to distinguish a positive statement from a negative one. Older people know that there is sense in the contradictory statements in the Bible and in the proverbs. They accept more readily the view that love and hate are not always opposites, and that bold self-assertion may indicate inward shyness. They have learned that the statement "I'm not worrying about it" may mean that the person is worrying about it, and that Portia's remark, "There's something tells me—but it is not love,—" means that it *is* love. The slip of the tongue which follows makes this quite clear.* Hence they find Freud's

---

* Beshrew your eyes,
They have o'erlooked me, and divided me:
One half of me is yours, the other half yours,—
Mine own, I would say . . .⁷⁷

surprising discoveries about the unconscious mind less difficult to believe.

I have given many classes in psychology and always found that my carefully chosen examples of dreams, slips of the tongue and other lapses, made little impression at first on students of any age, but when one found an example for himself he was always much impressed and thought that if I would only use his example, everyone would be convinced. I think the best way to help teachers to understand the unconscious mind as it concerns them will be to discuss some of the school subjects individually, and see what suggestions we have to offer.

Art

When one goes to an exhibition of children's art, one is surprised by the very high standard of the work and the realization that almost every picture was painted from a visual image. In other words, the intellect is in abeyance, and the unconscious mind (the dream mind) has produced the picture which the child copies onto the drawing paper. A visit to the school during the drawing lesson shows the children are concentrating intensely on their work and have great pleasure in doing it.

I have already quoted Blake's statement of how he worked, and here is Emerson writing on a related theme more than 120 years ago.

> We may owe to dreams some light on the fountain of this skill; for as soon as we let our will go and let the unconscious states ensue, see what cunning draughtsmen we are! We entertain ourselves with wonderful forms of men, of women, of animals, of gardens, of woods and of monsters, and the mystic pencil wherewith we then draw has no awkwardness of inexperience, no meagreness or poverty; it can design well and group well; its composition is full of art, its colors are well laid on and the whole canvas which it paints is lifelike and apt to touch us with terror, with

tenderness, with desire and with grief. Neither are the artist's copies from experience ever mere copies, but always touched and softened by tints from this ideal domain.[22]

This is intuitive knowledge of what Freud discovered many years later by his scientific interpretation of dreams.

We are all visualizers, as we know from our dreams, but many adults have lost the power in their waking life. Visual imagery can get in the way of scientific or logical thinking, and many of us have repressed it so successfully that we no longer realize such a thing exists. But most children visualize easily. If a child can form, and hold, a visual image of a shop, a street scene, a group of trees, a vase of flowers, his mother's face, or anything else, he has a perfect picture. The grouping cannot be wrong, for the unconscious mind must integrate in order to hold. If there should happen to be railings in his visual picture, the foreshortening will be perfect. The child need know nothing intellectually about foreshortening, all he has to do is to copy what he sees. If he sees his mother's face and paints it, he will paint his love of his mother as well as her face. *Every child's vision is real art,* and even if the representation of the vision is inexpertly done the picture will appear effective, especially at a distance. I once saw at the back of a classroom, a picture of a playground scene. I went up to see it and found to my surprise that not a single child was explicitly drawn. There were some lines and dabs of color as if the artist had drawn in hurriedly the highlights of her vision, but the grouping was perfect and the picture most "real."

It is no wonder, therefore, that some teachers who cannot themselves draw can get beautiful pictures from the children, while other teachers, some with good art training but who make no use of the unconscious mind, are unsuccessful. The surprising influence of the dream mind will be

[84]

immediately observable in some of the pictures. A shy little boy may draw the adults much too big; he sees them like that and the teacher would spoil the picture if he got the boy to correct the mistake. A too-long arm may mean grasping after someone, an ear too big may mean listening; professional cartoonists draw this way sometimes. Emotions will be indicated by remarkable subtleties of gesture or expressions.

It is a help at first if the teacher can see a good picture in his mind's eye and describe it to the children. An accomplished teacher I know would describe, say, an old lady who was sitting opposite her in a corner seat of the train. "She must have been tired, for she was asleep. Her hands were together on her lap. She was wearing [here a few vivid details about her dress]. Now, close your eyes and see if you can see that old lady. Can you see her? Well, draw her, just as you see her." This steadies the image for the children and trains them to hold images of their own later.

The richness of our visual and dream images can only be realized by one who understands Freud's work. If you have ever talked about dreams with a psychoanalyst you will have discovered how meaningful some of the "details" in the dream really are. It is these deeper meanings which give the value to art. We are surrounded by beauty, but we don't see it. The artist chooses a bit of it, his dream mind eliminates the inessentials, and we then see the beauty which we had missed before. Art should lead us to appreciate the beauty of life. To run away from life and take refuge in art is, I think, a weakness. That is why it is good to draw common everyday subjects which the children understand: the men digging up the road, a local shop, a cinema queue, a bowl of fruit, a vase of flowers, a country scene in sunshine, rain, or snow. It is not exact representation we want, but the *spirit* of the thing, and this is what the dream mind will give. Every good artist is painting more than he realizes, as every inspired poet, novelist, or dramatist puts meanings into his work which he knows nothing about. "Was it really I who wrote that?" Voltaire is said to have exclaimed as he sat in the loge watching his own play. George Eliot declared that while she was writing *Adam Bede,* it was "as though another mind had taken possession of her pen and guided it."[7]

This method of art teaching has great importance for another reason; the unconscious has many unused "drives" which are calling for expression. It contains repressed material which is also calling for expression. All this material tends to take a visual form, and often causes troublesome dreams. If we turn these visions into pictures, we have given the material a run in real life, as it were, and the outflow has relieved tension. Much of our present-day mental illness is due to mental tension which might have been relieved by art work of this kind.

Music and Speech

"The sensations and ideas thus excited in us by music, or expressed by the cadences of oratory, appear from their vagueness, yet depth, like mental reversions to the emotions and thoughts of a long past age."[14] I wish I could quote the whole long passage from Darwin's *The Descent of Man,* for it explains many problems. Darwin traces music and impassioned speech back to the season of courtship of our animal ancestors. At that time animals of all kinds are excited not only by love, but by the strong passions of jealousy, rivalry, and triumph. Darwin thought the musical intervals used to express these emotions have come down to us by inheritance and been modified and complicated as evolution proceeded. We are all aware of sex tunes, and the interest they have for young people. Both popular and classical composers often make use of what we may call the "mother complex" theme; the intervals the baby uses in crying, and the intervals the mother uses in comforting a baby. Wagner and others make frequent use of aggressive themes, and songs of triumph are indeed common.

Music is in the unconscious all right, but it has to be evoked. Children whose musical mothers sang to them tend to appreciate music. Children who have never had music associated with their emotions may have no interest in it. One cannot, of course, evoke and deal with all one's rich heritage, but if we are going to try to interest children in music we should begin in a *simple* way in order to get back to the unconscious mind, as I have suggested earlier.

This is how Miss Greenwood did it in East London. I quote from her letter.

A happy infants school is pervaded with music. It enters spontaneously into almost everything, even writing. The children I had, loved the rhythmic swinging along of letter formations to suitably timed and well-accented tunes which they hummed or sang as they wrote or made their writing patterns. For example: a succession of intertwining loops to "The Ash Grove;" a succession of u's, t's m's, or p's to "The Keel Row;" a succession of o's to "Hush-a-Bye Baby;" of e's to "Poor Jenny is a-Weeping;" of a's to "Fire Down Below;" of h's to "Eine Kleine Nachtmusik;" of w's to Brahms's Waltz 15, and so on, to bits of classics—even symphonies! Children wrote beautifully in my pre-war school, not the cramped tight style taught by the junior staff. A short rhythmic practice once a day was quite enough, just a few minutes.

Rhythm and time should come before tune. *A first stage* which continued throughout all classes was *spontaneous* tripping, dancing, running, marching, percussion bands. (Lucky the infants school where there are good pianists!) The children absorbed the whole

[87]

feel of music into their beings, they loved it from the start. Simultaneously and unconsciously they are feeling time.

Singing at all stages, nursery rhymes, songs—heaps—as many as possible. These can be taken dramatically, as in your example of the teaching of the sea shanty [page 89]. Tone comes unconsciously and any polish, later.

Notes. Continue progress with conscious listening to notes. Walk them, march them, clap them, name them. Children could walk or march to represent crotchets, they could run to represent quavers, they could trip to represent half notes and one and one-half notes, and they could march slowly to represent minums. The semi-breve would be the long, slow, old grandfather note. We had large sheets with printed notes on and named, and the children could see what they were doing. It's all done simultaneously, easily, it is no burden.

Simple Time. It creates the rhythmic beat, makes music easier to read—they will understand this. Introduce the bar and time signatures. Write bars with four crotchets, eight quavers, and other combinations of notes. Introduce beats, emphasizing the first. Mark it as they walk or run, with a stamp or a clap. Let them conduct.

Tune. Show the places of notes on the staff, first the simple scale, then very simple tunes. This leads to keys and key signature, and to sharps and flats. No bass until senior school.

Tone from the piano or other instrument. This can all be done easily in the infants school. I don't think it wise to muddle them with tonic solfa until they understand the scale. I should introduce tonic solfa in the lower classes of the junior school.

This, of course, is an exceptionally good beginning, but most junior school teachers cannot count on preparations of this kind. They have to begin in another way.

An experienced teacher, engaged on the training of teachers, was asked by his students to show them how to give a singing lesson. As the pupils would be strange to him, and many would not be interested in singing, he prepared the approach carefully. He thought a sea shanty would be a good beginning. He went to the school to see if a picture of a big sailing ship could be obtained, and was lucky enough to find a model of the "Cutty Sark" which he borrowed along with the rope used for tug-of-war games. In his lesson he showed the pupils the model first, told them about the tea clippers, their races for the markets, the many changes of sail necessary and the shantyman's songs to keep the sailors in time when, for example, they were hoisting sail. Then getting some of the boys to act as the sailors pulling the rope, he sang to them "Blow the Man Down" while the boys pulled in time. This was good fun, it had taken only a little time, and now the boys all wanted to learn the song. A simple start, of course, but then fast progress with future lessons because the unconscious minds were functioning freely.

In learning to read music, the solfa approach is very useful. I once saw a brilliant teacher take a class of 120 boys he had never seen before, and who had never attempted to read music, and teach them to read a two-part song in one hour. He had a short pointer, and he began by saying, "Tell me how many beats I make," and he tapped the desk four times. He wrote on the board a bar of solfa notation with four d's and said "Sing these four notes like this." He illustrated, pointing to the notes, and the children sang them. "Now just as you can divide an apple into two equal parts, you can divide a beat into two equal parts. Put up your hand when you hear the half-beats." He went on beating steadily for a time until all the jerky hands had settled down, then he introduced half beats occasionally until all the children put their hands up at the right time. He wrote on the board underneath the first bar of solfa notation, another bar with half-beats in the second space, and got the class to sing this.

Then he explained that just as you can divide an apple into three quarters and a quarter, you can divide a beat into three quarters and a quarter. "Hands up when I beat three quarters and a quarter." He beat steadily for a time, then introduced half-beats. "No, no. These are half-beats. Don't you hear them saying it? 'Beats, beats, half-beats, beats.' Hands up when you hear three quarters and a quarter." The tapping pointer had never stopped, and the children almost hypnotized. He beat half-beats occasionally until all the jerky hands had stopped, then he introduced three quarters and a quarter several times, then half-beats again, and shook his head as a few hands went up. Soon he had all the time intervals which he required for the song well taught. By similar step-by-step methods he taught the tune intervals on the modulator, taking care that a wrong interval was never sung.

When attempting to read the song, he got the children to read the notes and sing them *in a monotone,* concentrating entirely on the *time.* This, strangely enough, does not weaken in the least the correct reading of the tune intervals, as a misreading would, and it enables any boy who had lost the place to pick it up again. Having got the time intervals secure, he revised on the modulator the tune intervals which might give trouble, and then the pupils read the song slowly. The whole lesson was as perfect as Wisdom's Arithmetical Dictation, and all the children were interested and striving for the full hour.

Voice production is another striking example of inherited skill. Every normal baby is born with perfect voice production. Notice the way he makes use of his full lung power; listen to the resonance from the cavities above the mouth; note how he tunes the mouth resonator to the pitch of the note he is using; look at the open throat, and the tip of the tongue tensed to give a ringing note. No wonder his voice can carry on for hours and penetrate brick walls, without a trace of voice strain. Even his softer notes would be heard at the back of the Albert Hall, as Caruso's and Gigli's were.

Why does the child lose that good voice? A succession of colds leaves mucous in the nasal cavities and this, in time, blocks them. Then "color," as the experts call it, is lost. He is told to speak softly, then the full lung power goes out of practice. He learns the rapid speech of our civilization, and the muscles of the lips, tongue, and throat tire with so much movement, and some of them cease to function. This does not matter in speaking softly, especially with people who do not mind slovenly speech, but it then becomes increasingly difficult to use the full voice. And what is the remedy? Let the children take part in plays and speak clearly to the back of the hall. Give them opportunities to read aloud. Let them sing often. Voice training is difficult enough when a professor has one pupil, and a teacher can hardly cope with thirty or forty pupils at once, even if he knows a lot about the subject. But some of the original power can often be regained if opportunities are provided. Tape recorders are very useful, both for letting the children hear good speech and for letting them realize how much better their own speech could be. Children are good mimics. Let them become interested in speech, and hear good speech, and they will copy it.

Composition

There are still many teachers who think good writing has to be "built up." They teach pupils to write in short sentences and get the full stops right, then to write longer sentences, and hope ultimately to introduce similes and metaphors to ornament the writing. This is the intellectual approach. But the unconscious mind can produce such wonderful writing that no writer of any repute would let his intellect interfere while creative work was in progress.

He keeps his intellect as a critical faculty to be used when the creative work is finished. Robert Graves expresses it very well:

> Many poets of my acquaintance have . . . also observed that on laying down their pens after the first excitement of composition they feel the same sort of surprise that a man finds on waking from a "fugue," they discover that they have done a piece of work of which they never suspected they were capable; but at the same moment they discover a number of surface defects which were invisible before.[51]

So does John Galsworthy: "The vitality and freedom of character creation derives, as a rule, from the subconscious mind instinctively supplying the conscious mind with the material it requires."[12] So too, Robert Louis Stevenson:

> And for the Little People, what shall I say they are but just my Brownies, God bless them! who do one-half my work for me while I am fast asleep, and in all human likelihood, do the rest for me as well, when I am wide awake and fondly suppose I do it for myself. That part which is done while I am sleeping is the Brownies' part beyond contention; but that which is done when I am up and about is by no means necessarily mine, since all goes to show the Brownies have a hand in it even then. Here is a doubt that much concerns my conscience. For myself—what I call I, my conscious ego, the denizen of the pineal gland unless he has changed his residence since Descartes, the man with the conscience and the variable bank-account, the man with the hat and boots, and the privilege of voting and not carrying his candidate at the general elections—I am sometimes tempted to suppose he is no story-teller at all, but a creature as matter of fact as any cheese-monger or any cheese, and a realist bemired up to the ears in actuality; so that by that account, the whole of my public fiction should be the single-handed product of some Brownie, some Familiar, some unseen collaborator whom I keep locked in a back garret, while I get all the praise and he but a share (which I cannot prevent him getting) of the pudding.[79]

I could quote similar statements from a seemingly endless number of creative people, but I will limit myself to mentioning Arthur Koestler's *The Act of Creation*[64] and L. L. Whyte's *The Unconscious Before Freud*,[85] two of many books which are excellent on the subject of creativity and the unconscious mind.

Of course teachers are not dealing with forty poets or forty novelists, but they should recognize the fundamental truth of their views and let the children write in peace. Teachers know they cannot themselves write a good report if they are interrupted every few minutes, yet so many destroy the peace of the classroom with their audible comments. When children write freely and from interest, their language is usually remarkably good. There are mistakes in spelling, grammar, and punctuation, to be sure, but these are easily remedied if hints are given *without discouraging the children*. Young children often write long sentences with many "ands." One could explain that one needs a pause in reading, and suggest that a sentence a page long should be changed to two sentences of half a page each, that is, work from the too large sentences to the correct size, not from the too small sentence. The large sentence will keep the "tune;" the short sentence seldom has a tune, and combined short sentences will have the words all out of step. The unconscious mind will supply suitable rhythms and all the similes and metaphors required. It tends, when feeling is strong, to run to poetry; all dreams are full of symbolism.

An infants mistress in an East End school had unusual skill in getting good compositions from her infants. The following essay was one of dozens I had at that time. The child was seven and one-half and the home conditions can be judged from the essay. If the reader will mentally add a few full stops and commas for the little girl, it will be seen that the writing is beautifully balanced, the "tunes" are just right and help to carry the message.

Our House

When you go to brabazon Street look up at our house you will
see white curtains and then look at the number if the number is
61 it is our house. We have only 2 rooms but we do not [?mind]
in the front room we have 2 beds and a sofa and a bed we sleep
on the sofa dad mum and john sleep on the bed dad has to get up
at 6 oclock in the morning and as soon as he gets the [?breakfast]
he begins to do his work he do not leave his work until 5 oclock
at night now I must tell you something sad about my house our
baby had to go in Hospital and they sent her out to quick it was
on a Fogy day to she had to go back and she had to stay in and
while she was in there she rolled up when mummy found out she
told us we were very sorry nearly all our aunts bought her a reiv
altogether there were 10 rievs and as I came along our street I
saw a funel come from our house.

This child is using the unconscious mind. She lets her
thoughts flow freely, as the great writers do; but if a
teacher marked every error in red ink, she could not write
like that again. I should praise her beautiful story and not
spoil it with comments and details. There will be more
suitable opportunities of helping her.

Here are a few extracts from letters of nine-year-olds to a
retired headmistress.

Dear Miss Greenwood,

I am very glad that you came to our play yesterday. I thought
it was very kind of you to travel all that way just to see the
Nertiverty play of Jesus. I was glad to see you back to school
again. In our singing lessons I had missed you singing lots of
songs. At dinner time on thursday just when the bell had gone lots
of us ran up the stairs and we all said excitedly, "Miss Greenwood
is here, and I hope she is going to see our play, and we was all
very excited. . . .

Dear Miss Greenwood,

I hope you are having a lovely time, in your house by the sea.
Everything seems different now you have left. All the children
have missed you ever shuch a lot. I missed you too. . . .

[94]

Dear Miss Greenwood,

Miss Greenwood we were so pleased when we saw you coming up the stairs. We all shouted when we saw you and we were grateful you to come. . . .

Now that is good writing in spite of the mistakes; one has no doubt of the sincerity of the welcome. The sentences ng of love, and go to the heart of the reader.

One word of warning: if a young teacher reading this carelessly thinks he has found a method of getting good compositions without the trouble of marking them, he is making a mistake. He will soon have compositions full of errors and getting steadily worse. If he is not going to give the same kindly attention to improving the child's work that a good headmaster would give to improving the young teacher's work, he will get nowhere with this method. The children will feel his indifference and lose interest in writing. Even if every care is taken he will have an occasional fluent writer whose contempt for spelling is too serious to ignore. He could say "I'm sorry, John, but I cannot understand your writing. Just write for five minutes today and I'll try to help you with your spelling." And a young teacher's composition books show steady deterioration instead of progress, he had better return to his red ink correcting until he has more experience.

Mathematics

In schools which work on formal methods, arithmetic a popular subject with the children, largely, I think, because they get to doing something themselves. The graded textbooks make the teaching easy, and many pupils sail along successfully and acquire much useful knowledge. It may surprise some teachers to know, however, that Lord Kelvin and his brother were doing differential and integral calculus at 11 years of age. Genius? Well, perhaps there was an innate factor, but knowing the life and work of their father, I think that if he had charge of one of our ordinary classes the pupils there would soon look like geniuses too.

H. G. Wells tells us that in one of his early teaching posts he

> threw out all the muddling-about with money sums, weights and measures, business "practice" and so forth that cumbered the teaching and examining of arithmetic, and took a class of small boys between six and eight straight away from the first four rules to easy algebra . . . for those days that was a bold thing to do. We got to fractions, quadratics and problems involving quadratics in a twelvemonth, and laid the foundation of two or three university careers by way of mathematics.[83]

It would be a bold thing to do even now; but now that we in England have changed to the metric system we shall not require to spend so much time on arithmetic, and it may be worthwhile to consider a more mathematical approach.

In many infants schools, the teaching of arithmetic has a better mathematical basis than the teaching in the junior departments. The infants play with one inch cubes, beads, beans, conkers, acorns, and learn the initial stage of counting in a thoroughly sound way. Some junior schools' staffs are impatient of the "playway" in the infants department, occasionally with justification, but more often because there is a tendency to regard ability to add and subtract hundreds, 10's, and units as being more important that number analysis. It is not always realized that it takes a child some time to distinguish *two* thing from one thing. The concept of *three* is another stage in development, and so on. One can teach a six year old how to add and subtract hundreds, 10's, and units, but he probably does not even understand the concept of 12. If h does not, he would be better employed learning in practical way that 12 is two sixes, three fours, four threes, or six twos.

Lack of mathematical ability is common. There is only one reason for it; bad teaching. If one is thinking of mathematics at the university level, there is, naturally, an important innate factor, but good teachers do not find this inability to understand mathematics unless the children have been hopelessly confused at the earlier stages by attempting sums they do not understand, and by hearing and using so many wrong answers to multiplication tables that it is almost impossible to teach the right answers. One should never ask aloud what eight sevens are, in case a child gives the wrong answer and all the class hear it.

Let us look at the better methods. Good infants schools have in addition to many one inch cubes, rods of one square inch sections, 10 units in length, and squares of wood, one inch thick, to show hundreds.

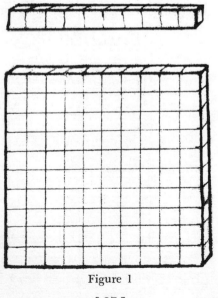

Figure 1

They have shops and weighing machines to learn abou money and weights and measures. Work of this kind give reality to the arithmetic. The junior schools should ha similar material to illustrate their work. They, too, shoul have one inch cubes. These could be used when require for number analysis and to explain the tables. They coul be used to show that $1 + 3 + 5 = 3^2$, $1 + 3 + 5 + 7 = 4$ and so on. A cube could be made with four to a side (6 cubes); lift off a layer from the top, one from the side an one from the adjacent side, and we have 3^3. Looking at th layers stripped off, a child can see that $4^3 = 3^3 + (4 \times$ $+ (4 \times 3) + (3 \times 3)$, and that $4^3 - 3^3 = 4^2 + (4 \times 3) + 3$ A few exercises of this kind would make it obvious tha $x^3 - y^3 = x^2 + xy + y^2$. By taking *two* layers off the to and so on, the x-y factor can be introduced to give th complete equation. $x^3 - y^3 = (x - y)(x^2 + xy + y^2)$.

The pupils could build up the tables on quarter inc squared paper, and then go beyond the 12 times by mear of Figures 2, 3, and 4:

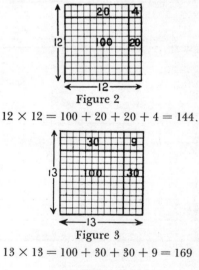

Figure 2

$12 \times 12 = 100 + 20 + 20 + 4 = 144.$

Figure 3

$13 \times 13 = 100 + 30 + 30 + 9 = 169$

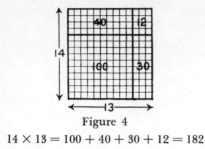

Figure 4

$14 \times 13 = 100 + 40 + 30 + 12 = 182$

nd so on. Smaller squares could be used for the larger umbers. Children visualize easily and can make good use f such diagrams. One famous engineer became so skilled y this method that he found it easier to multiply two iree-figure numbers mentally than by writing them down.

Junior school children should learn the relation of circumference and diameter by practical experiments, and be elped to understand the formula for the area of a circle y drawing a square on the radius. If the circle is enosed by four such squares they will see that the area is ss than $4r^2$ which will help them to remember it is $3\frac{1}{7}r^2$. rom the relation of circumference and diameter they can nd the area of a paper cylinder, and having that, can be own the diagram which Archimedes had inscribed on is tombstone, as one of his greatest discoveries, and find e area of a sphere (Figure 5). Pythagoras's theorem can e illustrated by squared paper (Figures 6, 7, 8).

Figure 5

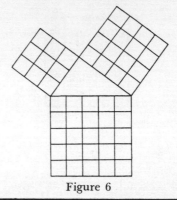

Figure 6

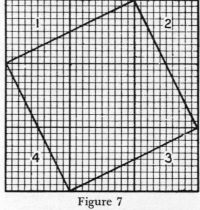

Figure 7

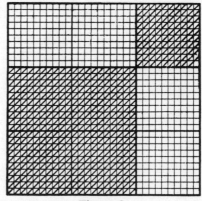

Figure 8

Modern books on mathematics will give the teacher many useful ideas if he looks for them, and the children can have a thrilling time with the subject.

Geography

When my youngest son was about five or six, I often put him to bed when I came home. "Tell me a story, daddy." "What about?" "Whales." I told him. Next night it was elephants. I had spoken about the oceans of the world when dealing with whales: the Greenland whale, the sperm whales of the warmer seas, the killer whales which had knocked Captain Scott's ponies off the ice in the Antarctic, and I had reached for the globe, of course. In dealing with elephants I had explained about the tropical forest region of Africa. "These are quite useful geography lessons," I said to myself. "I'll do the tropical grasslands tomorrow."

"Shall I tell you a story about antelopes tonight?" I asked hopefully. "No, I don't want to know about antelopes," the boy replied, and my nice sequence fell to pieces. "Well, what story shall I tell you tonight?" "What stories have you got?" "Oh! I could tell you about lions or tigers, bears, seals, monkeys, camels . . ." "What's a camel?" I did not expect that choice, but he learned something about the Sahara and other deserts.

Now this illustrates two aspects of what I consider a good lesson: I am apparently following the boy, and doing what he wants; but he is also following me, and doing what I want. I may appear to jump about from one subject to another, but I have in my own mind the symmetry of the climatic belts of Africa, for example, and I'll gradually teach that symmetry and the reasons for it as the boy can take it. The tremendous advantage of following the boy's wishes is that a child who *wants to know* anything, need only be told once. Repetition, question and answer,

revision, are all unnecessary. But let me define what
mean by *wanting* to know. A child may want to kno
things to please the teacher, or to pass an examination.
don't mean that kind of wanting. It is in the same catego
as the man who wants to save money, but neverthele
spends it, or the man who wants to give up smoking, ar
continues to smoke. It is the *unconscious* mind which ma
ters in wanting to know, not the conscious mind.

Here is a lesson I gave occasionally to junior pupils
demonstrate the method to the class teacher. I got a glo
and a big map of the world, and said to the class, "I'
going to take a geography lesson with you, boys and gir
What would you like me to tell you about? Africa, Am
ica, Australia, lions, tigers, elephants, kangaroos, or lo
birds? Any suggestions?" "Africa, sir." I gave my best ar
most suitable talk on Africa for two or three minut
"What next?" "Greenland, sir." I gave my best talk
Greenland for one or two minutes. "Tigers, sir." I ga
my best talk on India. "Budgerigars, sir." My best talk
Australia, and so on for 15 or twenty minutes. Then I sa
"Now could you write something about the lesson? A
part you like, but I can only give you five minutes. P
your name at the top of the sheet of paper, pencil will d
and don't worry about writing or spelling. I can read the
all right. Off you go."

I would give them 10 minutes if they were all writi
fast, as they usually were, for I had already broken do
many of their inhibitions. Then I asked them to bri
their papers out to me. I read them out to the class, pra
ing every effort. They were usually surprisingly good, a
some children had added information they had learn
from other sources. Some of the efforts would be poor,
course. Suppose a boy wrote "Elefants live in Greenlan
I should say, "You are interested in elephants, Joh

Good. They don't live in Greenland, however, it's too cold there. They live here, in Africa, or here, in India," and the boy would soon make progress.

Teachers who are well informed on geography could make use of a few lessons of this type to get the children interested and free, and then get them settled down to study and write books. Teachers who are not well enough informed to follow the children's requests could work through the class textbooks. They could give a talk about the subject with a globe and a large map, then let the children read about the subject for 10 or 15 minutes and then write about it. In the silent half hour the teacher could give some individual encouragement and a few hints or corrections. He should remember, however, that silence is essential, and he would be better to leave the correcting and walk slowly to where a nucleus of disorder was showing, than to bawl across the classroom at a troublesome pupil. It will be appreciated that the best approach is to try to get the pupil to gather, write about, and illustrate the geographical knowledge *he wants*. The influence of the teacher, the class, and the books will keep him in a useful track.

I should like to see more scientific geography taught, even in junior schools. It can be done so easily if it is done for short periods in the course of other lessons. A half-hour lesson on the movements of the earth would not be suitable for junior school pupils, but an occasional demonstration with a globe and a lamp would soon lead to an understanding. Let a few pupils in succession carry the globe round the light until no one makes the mistake of moving the axis from the imaginary North Star. Similarly, one could explain in a few five minute talks why it is hotter at the equator, and why there is rainfall there and not on the Sahara; why north and south of the forest region the vegetation grows quickly when the rain comes, and preserves its life in tough little seeds when the drought comes; why the Sahara Desert conditions move north over the Mediterranean countries in the summer, and so on. It is quite wrong to think junior pupils can only take stories about children of other lands, or a few simple facts. That is all they can take if their powerful unconscious minds are excluded, but let the unconscious minds function freely, and the children are as clever as we are.

History

Emerson thought history should be read with something of a personal approach. History was made by our ancestors, we are epitomes of our ancestors, and vestiges of all they thought and did are in our own unconscious minds. We can understand the noble figures in history because something of that nobility is in our own inheritance, and if we are honest with ourselves we shall recognize the wickedness we read about as the result of tendencies which we too inherited, even if we have been fortunate enough to have left most of them latent in our unconscious minds. In Emerson's essay on "History" we find: "This remedies the defect of our too great nearness to ourselves. This throws our actions into perspective—and as crabs, goats, scorpions, the balance and the waterpot lose their meanness when hung as signs in the zodiac, so I can see my own vices without heat in the distant persons of Solomon, Alcibiades, and Catiline."[23]

Historical knowledge built into walls brick by brick by the intellect, as if the knowledge had nothing to do with the historian himself, is not the best kind of knowledge. It is not this kind of man who makes the original or important contributions to the subject, or gets real pleasure from it. No historian can know all history, and his interest should guide him in making the selection. As Emerson said in the same essay, "The fact narrated must correspond to something in me to be credible or intelligible." Now would it not be possible to allow the child's real interest to guide us more in what we teach, instead of trying to stick "interest" on to what we prescribe for him? There is this weakness in our present system, that it is very ineffective. Apart from the pupils who are taking history as an examination subject in Grammar Schools, very little history is known by school children. We joke about the "memorable dates" 55 B.C. and 1066, but it is too near the truth to be a laughing matter.

Professor M. V. C. Jeffreys, formerly at Birmingham University, maintained many years ago that the history we try to teach the children is a "conglomerate" which they cannot understand. By dividing history into "periods" we cut the longitudinal strands of history, and school children can never find any real sequence in it. He thought we should begin with some of the longitudinal strands: the history of transport, of ships, sea battles, houses, clothes, and so on. There are so many of these strands that one of them would surely interest the child.

Many museums have beautiful dioramas of the history of transport and the history of lighting. There are models of the early railway engines, motor cars, motor bicycles, airplanes, sailing ships, warships, and other interesting objects. Colored postcards or diagrams are available, which could be bought by the children to illustrate their original books. Young boys could begin with the history of the airplane, motor car, or railway engine, and follow on with the history of transport or ships. These would give a preliminary sweep through history, the study would have sequence and come up to the present-day objects with which they are familiar. Girls may prefer to begin with the history of clothes, or the house, and suitable cheap books are now on the market with many colored pictures. These could be copied or cut out to illustrate the child's book. To be the author of a book on history is a great encouragement to the children, and once the unconscious mind is engaged, progress is rapid. The boys would see themselves paddling the dug-out canoe, learning to use a sail, inventing the steam engine and the paddle wheels, and so on; they evoke and develop the inherited knowledge of what their ancestors did, and so enrich their own personalities. To return to Emerson, "Education often wastes its effort in attempts to thwart and balk this natural magnetism, which is sure to select what belongs to it."[21]

If the more orthodox books are used, I think teachers should try to give *richer* lessons than they usually do, and let the pupils *select* what they will write about. Talk for about a third of the time, let the children read about the subject for another third, then let them write about it. That would leave a silent time, when the teacher could be giving some individual encouragement and help in a quiet voice, the children's ears would be rested, and they would be ready for the next oral lesson. A headmaster has an immediate check on what is going on with this free work in a class. He has only to look at a few of the children's books. If the written work is getting steadily better and more valuable, success is assured. If it is not, it should be stopped, and another attempt with better preparation made later.

Physical Education and Handwork

When Madame Montessori heard of the new school desks designed to prevent spinal curvature, she expressed her indignation as follows: (I quote from memory.) "The spinal column, the most primitive part of the organism, which was adequate when man fought the desert lion and hewed the solid rock to his uses, bends and cannot resist the yoke of the school!"

We have, indeed, moved a long way from the days when we began to remedy this state of affairs with some "physical jerks" once or twice a week, but there is no doubt that in many schools children still sit at desks for much longer than is good for them. It is one of the benefits of the educational methods we advocate, that this does not happen. Physical exercises and games now form part of the work in most schools, and great improvements in the methods of teaching have taken place. One or two fundamental points may, however, be worth mentioning. Children could get pleasure and valuable exercise from climbing a hill, but not from climbing a treadmill, although the movements are similar. Freud found that stimulation and inhibited response to it tends in time to cause hysteria, and that activity without stimulus tends to cause mental and physical exhaustion. This is obvious from a consideration of the sex instinct, but it applies to all reflex and instinctive actions, and even to the more intellectual processes. Hence, play with balls, hoops, or skipping ropes, or happy activities in the gymnasium, tend to be more beneficial than physical exercises done to order.

I mentioned earlier the remarkable fact that all children are born with perfect voice production, and that most of them soon lose it. Another remarkable fact is that many young children walk beautifully, with a perfect contrabody movement, the hips turning one way and the shoulders the other way at every step. This brings the big muscles of the trunk into play, and gives more power, a longer stride, and a rhythmic movement which does not tire the body easily. It is not long, however, before young children are riding little tricycles, and bicycles—a useful training, of course, for this age of wheeled transport—but this is one of the causes of the increased use of the knee movements in walking and the loss of the contra-body movements.

I once took the chair at a lecture given by a Greek ballet dancer. He was very tall and muscular, and from my chair behind him, I noticed his very flexible body. I mentioned this to him later. "Yes," he said, "we joke among ourselves about the rigid British spine." It is no doubt imposing to see our troops marching with their rigid spines, swinging their arms artificially, as the arms would swing naturally if the contra-body movement was used. One hopes they loosen up a bit in the long marches and save their energy. It may be, of course, the heavy equipment soldiers have to carry makes a swinging walk undesirable, but there is no reason why our children should not be encouraged to walk properly.

Much physical damage is caused because many people do not yet understand the changes that take place when the body goes on a "War footing," as it is called. W. B. Cannon has explained for us the wonderful mechanisms the body has for dealing with emergencies.[8] When danger threatens us we feel the emotions of fear or rage, and for our animal and savage ancestors, this situation usually meant fast running to escape, or fierce fighting to survive. Either fear or rage immediately releases into the blood stream a small amount of adrenalin from the suprarenal glands (two small glands, one above each kidney). Even very small amounts of adrenalin in the blood cause the following changes to take place: (a) The rate of heart beat is increased. This speeds up the circulation of the blood, bringing more oxygen to the muscles and carrying away more quickly the waste products of muscular action, (b) More red corpuscles are released into the blood stream

[108]

from the spleen. This amplifies (a) above, (c) The rate of respiration is increased. Hence, again, more oxygen, and quicker removal of the waste products of muscular action, (d) Much of the blood supply is withdrawn from the digestive system and the reproductive system; for example, the mouth becomes dry. These "civilian" activities can wait, (e) An increased supply of blood is sent to the big muscles of the legs and arms. This will increase their strength and help sustain it, (f) Part of the reserve of blood sugar in the liver is released into the blood stream. This again gives a considerable increase in physical energy, (g) The hair on the body becomes erect. This increases the apparent size of the animal, and makes it more dangerous looking. In many animals the teeth are bared, the claws protruded and other preparations made for attack. In human beings the little hairs of the body become erect, giving "goose flesh." (In the safer conditions of civilization the "snarl" is often toned down to a "sneer" or even further to a "sardonic smile" but even the "sardonic smile" is a tentative baring of the eye teeth, and is unconsciously understood as such by the observer.) and, (h) The composition of the blood is changed so that it congeals more quickly. This is a great advantage in case of injury.

These changes take place as a result of impulses from the thalamic region of the brain, one of the oldest parts, which we have in common with the animals. The cerebral cortex, which we have greatly in excess of the animals, has little power to influence these internal changes.[9] If we feel fear or rage the body prepares for "war," and the "civilian" activities are shut down. No wonder then, that overworked people get duodenal ulcers. If there is food in the stomach when we become anxious or alarmed, it will stay there, and no gastric juice will be released to digest it until the anxiety ceases. Here then is another reason for the freer, happy schooling which we advocate. A bullying teacher, with his cane handy, can put the normal bodily mechanisms of his more nervous pupils out of action, and possibly cause permanent injury to some of them.

An interesting detail from Cannon's work is the explanation of "second wind." As the animal becomes out of breath from fighting or running, this state causes a further release of adrenalin into the blood stream, and the animal or man is quickly refreshed. "What rest will do only after an hour or more, adrenalin will do in five minutes or less."[10] Athletes know that they can run faster or jump higher when they "have the needle" as they call it. That is, when their interest and excitement have evoked these changes. There is no harm in using these extra powers for short periods. The lion does not suffer from the attack on its prey, nor does the antelope suffer when it has successfully evaded the lion. The "civilian" activities soon take their place again. Human beings, however, often suffer sustained fear or anxiety, and it is the prolongation of the state of "war" which can have harmful results. Another interesting detail is that an injection of adrenalin will cause all these changes in the body to take place, but the subject will not feel fear or rage. He can describe quite calmly what is happening to his feelings.

An important part of physical education is *handwork*. When our primitive ancestors adopted the upright posture and released the hands, there was a rapid development of the mental powers, and there is still a close relationship between the development of the hands and mental development. I published some years ago a case of a boy of six who could not talk at all, and was only learning to walk. On questioning the parents, the astonishing fact came to light that the child had been tied hand and foot almost continually since he was six weeks old. He was a normal baby, who had been circumcised when he was six weeks old. On medical advice his hands were tied to stop him touching the affected part. Then eczema developed, and the tying was continued to stop him scratching the eczema. The eczema continued and got worse, and the tying up was continued. The parents had done their best to develop speech, but it would not develop. We recommended the removal of all restrictions, and the child at last began to make progress. The following were some of the conclusions:

> The case seemed to us to be important as helping to throw light on the question whether or not intelligence can be regarded as an innate quality. It seems possible that this child of six, whose intelligence was inferior to that of a child of two years old, may have been hindered in development almost entirely by the drastic restrictions made to his movements.

> One does not require to embrace the behaviorists' views to agree that speech is to some extent "conditioned conduct," and that the use of the senses is essential for the development of intelligence. If it could be shown that mental retardation followed restricted movements in infancy, then the widely held view that we can ignore the environment of the first few years and still measure innate intelligence would be shown to be unsound.

> H. S. Jennings has shown that many animal traits usually regarded as due to inheritance, only happen to be constant because the environment is constant.[62] It may be that what we regard as average intelligence is only average because of an average bad environment, and that the Kelvins and Darwins represent another possible average. This is a view held by many of the psychoanalysts.[59]

This was an extreme case, to be sure, but it is a great mistake to keep the brighter pupils on intellectual work and omit handwork, as if it was an activity suitable only for the future "hewers of wood and drawers of water." There is more to human development than intellectual ability. We have too many children in our child guidance clinics who have a high intelligence quotient but no common sense. Handwork which interests children develops common sense and many other valuable qualities. It was with great pleasure that I first saw children in infants schools using good quality saws and hammers, and making little models for themselves. This joyous activity went on for an hour every day, and I never heard of any serious accident; chisels were not used of course. The standard of reading, writing, and arithmetic in these schools was, not surprisingly, a high standard.

Chapter Seven

Some General Problems

WHEN APPEALS ARE MADE to the unconscious mind the procedure in marking the written work has to be changed. I shall mention first how the marking should be done, and then explain why the traditional procedure is unsuitable.

The Marking of Books

The pupil's book should be treated as one would treat a friend's manuscript if criticism had been invited. One would not put red ink or blue pencil on it. Comments would be made verbally, or in soft lead pencil which could easily be rubbed out, and there would not be too many of them. No headmaster would tell a young teacher *all* his faults at once lest he discourage him, and the same rule applies to the child's creative work. Guidance and encouragement should be given, of course, but one or two hints or corrections per page are usually sufficient.

One *suggests* changes to an author. The author need not take them, and he may know best, even if he is a child. A teacher can spoil the music of a composition if he is not careful, and in good writing *the tune* carries the meaning as well as the words. I once wrote in a book for children, "And these ancestors of ours were almost animals

[113]

and always hungry." The publisher's reader changed this to, "And these ancestors of ours were not very different from animals and often hungry." He thought his version was more accurate, but he had ruined my tune. It is astonishing what suitable tunes even infants use when they write freely. If a child is writing a diary, I should *ask* him if I may see his diary, and I should be even more careful of criticizing what he had written, although I should try to help.

Now this procedure contradicts the traditional views about marking books. What a fuss Heads and inspectors used to make if all errors in the written work were not corrected! And with good reason. Mistakes uncorrected tended to become permanent; the children lost interest in the work and it gradually deteriorated. If all errors were carefully corrected in red ink, and if the child wrote the correct version three times, spelling improved, and progress was made. But it was slow progress. The markings of one set of compositions took two or three hours of the teacher's free time, and one written composition a week was about all he could allow. When children are allowed to write freely on several subjects every day, and only some of the mistakes are corrected, how will the spelling and grammar improve?

It does improve, because the *unconscious mind quickly perceives relationships*. This is one of the characteristics of genius. Newton sees a relationship between the falling apple and the moon's movements; Watt relates the pressure of steam on the kettle lid with the pressure on the piston of the pump; Kekulé relates the snake in his dream, seizing its own tail and whirling round, with the formula he was seeking for benzene. In the same way the child quickly relates the correctly spelled word he sees in the course of his reading, with the incorrect spelling he has used in his book, and puts this right. But there must be *personal interest* in one's writing; the *unconscious* mind must be functioning. If a boy is writing *to please the teacher* he will not see these distant relationships.

Sir Cyril Burt told me many years ago that at a psychological conference a psychiatrist, Dr. X., said in the course of his address, "My first patient was an alcoholic." At a meeting on the following day a speaker, who had evidently not been at the first meeting, said, "I have the honor to be Dr. X's first patient." Sir Cyril related the two remarks, but saw not a sign that anyone else in the group had, and on inquiry found that only one person besides himself had related the two statements. The intellect does not look for links of this kind; the unconscious does.

Again, if the boy has written *to please the teacher* he wants the teacher to look at his work carefully. He likes to see red ink on his book. An author would hate it on his manuscript. This difference is seen whenever we compare mechanical learning with learning from interest. I should never ask a child to spell a word aloud in case he spelled it wrongly and all the class heard the wrong spelling. I should never ask questions about tables for the same reason. Teachers will remember that when they first marked compositions and corrected spellings, they soon had to look at the dictionary to see how the words *were* spelled. On the other hand, if a baby hits one cheek and then the other with a spoon, I should not interfere. He will find the way to the mouth all right, and not lose it again. Similarly a child can make mistakes in trying to climb a tree without the mistakes becoming permanent. And if he is writing a book and wants to make a success of it, he will soon learn to spell.

Discipline

So far I have been suggesting that education should be a pleasurable process, and some Heads may be wondering if this is good character training. Thomas Huxley said that perhaps the most valuable result of education was the ability to do what had to be done, when it had to be done, whether one liked it or not.[60] Some school children learn this lesson from teachers or prefects with canes. Where do the happy pupils learn it, for it is an important lesson?

Strangely enough, they learn it quite easily in the course of their work. No one can write a good original book, for example, without encountering plenty of difficulties; pictures or diagrams won't fit, or won't stick, or they smudge the writing; the textbook or encyclopedia is difficult to understand; one cannot write nicely or spell correctly, and so on. In perfecting these skills the children become competent workers who can take difficulties in their stride, and can give sustained attention to any task. Also, by using the unconscious mind, one is more in harmony with others, for the unconscious mind is common to all. The personality of the child is functioning freely. He is not troubled by feelings of injustice, anger, revenge, jealousy, or "martyrdom." He is always willing to help others, because he identifies himself with others.

Of course, as all teachers know very well, love will not do everything in obtaining good discipline. Man has a bit of the wolf in him, and if the leader of the pack shows any weakness, the young ones will challenge his leadership, and take great pleasure in pulling him down. Those of us who went from teaching to the training of teachers were very puzzled at first to know why students had so much difficulty in keeping discipline. I remember, for example, taking over a class from a student because it was getting out of hand, settling the children for him, and getting out of the way again, and in a minute or two they were in disorder again. Yet he was teaching quite nicely. I had moved to the back of the class, and suddenly I said to myself, "I've got it! He is *not looking* at the children!" I had done this for years as a teacher without knowing it. It was something I had learned unconsciously in handling difficult classes.

Politicians, psychologists, and writers on education sometimes talk as if "a trained teacher" was a definite term. Yet any Head knows that some trained teachers are of the greatest possible value to the school and the community, while other trained teachers are of little use anywhere. In a school which has really good teachers the question of discipline does not arise. A first-class teacher would hesitate to spoil the nice tone of his class by bullying anyone. And, strange to say, there seem to be no difficult children in the classes he takes over. How is this?

Because from his first contact with the class he evokes love from the pupils. He does not make love to them in any way. His unconscious speaks to their unconscious, and they never misunderstand that. Then he has always something interesting to say to them, and he says this to every pupil, his eyes meeting their eyes every few seconds. They like this. If a boy misbehaves he holds the culprit with his eyes for a few seconds till he sits up and pays attention, but if that does not succeed, he carries on with his lesson and deals with the boy later. He does not want to interrupt his lesson and lose the attention of the others over one boy. He does not talk long before he gives the pupils something to read or write, so that they have a rest from his voice, and can get expression for what they have been listening to. In his supervision, he speaks quietly to the boy who has misbehaved and impresses on him that he won't stand any nonsense in the class. Yet again, the unconscious love speaks to the boy's unconscious love. If any further action is necessary when a lesson is in progress, he can quietly tell the boy to leave the class and stand up at the back, and leave him there for five or 10 minutes, which will seem like half an hour to the boy. With practically all the boys on the teacher's side and wanting to listen, what chance has a rebel?

A teacher of this type has many different techniques, learned rather by instinct and experience than by reading books. One of my students at King's College told me he was having trouble with discipline at the mixed Grammar School where he was practicing, and I went along to see him. I spoke to the headmaster first, of course, who said the student was hopeless. "Listen to the row going on now," he said. "That is his class at the far end of the corridor!" I went along to see the student, and told him to carry on for a time so that I could see his teaching. He taught a bit, scolded angrily, taught again, scolded again, and so on, finally came over to me and said, "I'm giving up teaching altogether, sir, I can't do it." "Nonsense," I said, "we've all had trouble with discipline at the beginning. You sit at the back and I'll take the class. Watch my eyes all the time, the eyes have a lot to do with it." And I began to teach.

The class was immediately quiet and interested. Soon a pretty girl in the front, who had been playing up the student, tried her tricks on me by interrupting my lesson with an irrelevant question. I looked at her disapprovingly, ignored her remark, and carried on with my lesson. After teaching for about 15 minutes, I gave the pupils some written work to do, and wandered round the desks, silently looking at what they were doing, or making a whispered comment. The behavior remained very good until the bell rang for dismissal.

I then had time for a talk with the student. He was very surprised at the change that had taken place, but although I had asked him to watch my eyes, he had missed most of the important points. He could not, of course, have noticed that I never once looked at the pupils while he was teaching. I pretended to be reading my notebook, and to be quite unconcerned about the behavior. But once I took over the class my eyes were all over the place. If I had looked at the children while they were misbehaving, and done nothing about it, my eye control would have been weakened. The student had noticed how I dealt with the pretty girl, but he had not noticed that in the supervision I had moved to her place and praised her good writing. I was determined to say a friendly word to her as soon as possible in case I had alienated her by my snub. Nor had he noticed that my looking at books was only a pretense, for I looked at everyone in the class every two or three seconds, and damped down several nuclei of disorder by watching the person concerned. When one small area looked dangerous I slowly walked along to that part of the class "supervising the written work" there. But all in silence. I had sacrificed the value of my supervision for the time being to bring this class back to good behavior.

I moved the student at once, of course, to an elementary school, where he would get some useful coaching, and he became quite good.

A teacher who looks like the leader of the pack, and sees everything that is going on in the class, all the time, can usually steady down children who are a little difficult. A class of hooligans is another matter, of course, and only an experienced teacher like the one mentioned in Chapter Two can get them into order by a series of clever psychological maneuvers. A master discharged from the army after being wounded in the first World War, got a post at a private school, and was asked by the headmaster to take a rowdy class that had already defeated several temporary teachers. The headmaster showed him to the class and left him. The boys all began to sing "Won't you come home, Bill Baily." The new master sat at his desk and listened calmly. This was no fun, so they soon stopped, and waited for him to say something so that they could rag him. When they were quiet he said, "You're a poor lot of singers. You don't even know the first verse. I'll write it on the board for you. Now let us hear it properly." They started again, "That's better. Now I'll write the second verse for you." It was soon the play interval, and they all rushed out, and soon rushed in again. He waited for a bit, and then said, "Let's start at the first verse again," and he gave them the note. But they did not want to sing. "Well, what do you want? Do you want me to teach you anything?" They did. And of course, he soon had them in hand with one of his most fascinating lessons, and his good eye control.

Lack of technical skill in handling a class can turn a kindly, loving teacher into an angry bully. It can spoil the teaching of the best informed teacher. We need to pay much more attention to discipline than we do. The psychology I should like teachers to remember for good discipline is this: (a) The unconscious mind is a storehouse of all the wisdom, skill, loving kindness, and wickedness of humanity. We can evoke either the "good" or the "bad" qualities by example and encouragement, and we can leave latent in the unconscious and more or less inactive, the qualities we do not want, (b) All the school subjects were developed by men who were interested in the subjects, that is, by men for whom these subjects were

[120]

sublimations of their instinctive lives. To learn them intellectually is of little value. Barristers have to do much intellectual learning in order to present their case at short notice, but they forget it all in a week. Good teachers arouse *instinctive* interest in what they are teaching, and it then becomes enjoyable and is remembered, and (c) Discipline is never good discipline until it comes because the children are serene and happy and interested in the work they are doing; but this can only be built up gradually. It is essential to learn how to control children by one's better presence, bold confidence, vigilance, and silence, for one often gets a class where nothing else would be effective except a cane. As love grows, and the tone of the class improves, the pupils can be left more and more without supervision, until the teacher can leave the room without the discipline being affected.

The Inheritance of Acquired Characters

Darwin introduced an important new factor to explain evolution, but he also attached great importance to the explanation that Lamarck had given. In the preface to the Second Edition of *The Descent of Man* he wrote,

> I may take this opportunity of remarking that my critics frequently assume that I attribute all changes of corporeal structure and mental power exclusively to the natural selection of such variations as are often called spontaneous; whereas, even in the first edition of the *Origin of Species* (1859), I distinctly stated that great weight must be attributed to the inherited effects of use and disuse, with respect both to the body and mind.[15]

Most modern biologists prefer to assume no inheritance of acquired characters, as this view is more in harmony with, for example, Weismann's discovery of the early separation of the sex cells from the soma. Freud found that the surprising new facts he was discovering would not fit into this hypothesis, and he had to assume inheritance to account for them. The unconscious minds of his patients from many different countries made use of symbols in such a remarkably uniform way, for example, that it almost seemed as if symbolism was a kind of prehistoric language we had been left with. Young children use these symbols before they have learned them from anybody.

The simplest explanation of instinct in animals is that they inherit the skill and knowledge of their ancestors. In no other way can we account for some of the remarkable migrations of birds and fish. The Bronze Cuckoo, for example, never sees its mother, is reared in New Zealand by foster parents, which are non-migratory, and finds its way 2,500 miles over the open sea to the Solomon and Bismarck Islands. The migration of eels from the rivers of Europe and America to the breeding ground in the Sargasso Sea, and the return of the young eels to the rivers of Europe and America is another striking example of inherited memory. Robert Ardrey in *The Territorial Imperative* tells us that the young eels with 115 vertebrae go to Europe, and those with 107 vertebrae go to America.[1] He also gives some remarkable examples of navigation by the Laysan albatross[2] and by the Manx Shearwater.[3] These birds seem to know their way about the oceans of the world as if by instinct.

Man, too, is an animal, and Freud's discoveries showed that instinctive knowledge is just as important for man as for animals. I quote some of the views he was compelled to adopt from the facts:

It seems to me, for instance, that symbolic connections, which the individual has never acquired by learning, may justly claim to be regarded as a phylogenetic heritage (1916-1917).[45]

[122]

I believe these *primal phantasies,* as I should like to call them, and no doubt a few others as well, are a phylogenetic endowment (1916-1917).[48]

. . . the man of prehistoric times survives unchanged in our unconscious (1915).[43]

Constitutional dispositions are also undoubtedly after-effects of experiences by ancestors in the past; they too were once acquired. Without such acquisition there would be no heredity (1916-1917).[47]

Mankind's ethical strivings, whose strength and significance we need not in the least depreciate, were acquired in the course of man's history; since then they have become, though unfortunately only in a very variable amount, the inherited property of contemporary men (1915).[43]

Sir Alister Hardy, Emeritus Professor of Zoology in the University of Oxford, gives a fascinating account of evolution in his book *The Living Stream.* He takes the view that the contributions of Lamarck and Samuel Butler have been undervalued in the past. Each had expressed an important aspect of the truth, and while we know much more about the problem now, Sir Alister thinks we have still much to learn about it. There may well be an internal factor which has so far eluded us.[52]

Mind and Intellect

Many people think that the mind and the intellect are the same thing. But the intellect is only part of the mind, and it developed late in evolution. It became increasingly important for man because of the wide range of his interests. It helps us to deal with situations for which our inherited knowledge and skill have not equipped us. The newly born duckling is mentally well equipped for the environment in which its ancestors lived, but it will swallow a cigarette end or a small piece of bright wire and kill itself; its ancestors were not familiar with such things. But think how successfully all wild life survives in spite of the many difficulties. It is no use dismissing the myriad mental processes involved in this survival by the word "instinct," as if the whole process was purely mechanical and as easily explained as a child's toy. "Instinct" in birds, animals, or men is the knowledge and skill which their ancestors acquired from long experience. "Habits are inherited," Darwin tells us.[16] Man has as much instinctual power as the animals have, and since Freud's discoveries we have come to realize that the intellect and the instinctual power are very like the rider and the horse. In fortunate circumstances there is harmony and all goes well, the horse providing the power and the rider the guidance. But other things can happen if the horse has not had some early training, or the rider has no consideration for the horse.

People who depend on their intellect and ignore the unconscious mind tend to lose their wisdom. I have been interested in the Hampstead Child Therapy Clinic since I retired. Several of the children who come there for treatment have very high I.Q.'s, one recently of 170. They have high intelligence, but some of them have no common sense. One boy of nine with an I.Q. of 159 had ill-treated a little girl during school and was sent to the headmistress. Asked why he had done such a thing, he said he thought it was funny. He got a severe scolding, two black marks were added to his record card, and he was dismissed in disgrace. He returned to the headmistress in five minutes and said "You know, I still think it was funny." A few more incidents of this kind and he was sent to the clinic, described as the most difficult boy the school ever had. A woman therapist helped to restore his balance and get him back to school again, but it was not an easy task.

As early as 432 B.C. Thucydides wrote "We have not acquired that useless over-intelligence which makes a man an excellent critic of an enemy's plans, but paralyzes him in the moment of action."[80] Wise men do not trust important decisions to their intellect. They "sleep on it," as they say; they allow the unconscious mind to have a look at it. It often happens that every logical reason points to one conclusion, yet the man has "a hunch" that that is not the right answer and one morning he wakens up with the correct solution. Elias Howe spent years trying to make a sewing machine, and always failed. He dreamed one night about savages carrying spears, through the blades of which were thongs of sinew. This gave him the solution to his problem, for he had been trying all these years to make a sewing machine with the eye of the needle in the head.[11] His conscious mind was too familiar with needles to see the obvious answer.

Now if this is getting complicated and somewhat remote from teaching, let me say at once that I am only mentioning these views so that we can return to the simple life with more confidence. What could be simpler than the approach to teaching that good infants mistresses make? They bring up and educate children as birds build nests and bring up young, without ever knowing how clever they are. In two or three years they teach 90 per cent of their children to read and write fluently, and give them an interest in knowledge and in life. They could not do this unless they were working largely by intuition, and making use of the unconscious minds of the children. I should like to see more of the infants approach carried forward into the junior and secondary schools. I have seen many infants teachers who, owing to war conditions, taught juniors or seniors, and they were all very successful. Of course there are infants teachers who could not do this,

I admit, but men and women who keep their instinctive lives undamaged, and make this the background for their behavior are very powerful personalities, and can hold their own quite effectively with the more intellectual people. Emerson, Somerset Maugham and many others have written to this effect. I shall quote one sentence from Somerset Maugham's *The Narrow Corner*. "She was a woman who had never read much, but she had a vast fund of knowledge, lying there like an unworked mine, gathered, you would have said, through innumerable generations out of the timeless experience of the race, so that she could cope with your book-learning and meet you on level terms."[68] Emerson, in his essay on "Manners," writes more fully to the same effect.[25] The power of the unconscious mind is almost unbelievable.

Culture

The concept of the unconscious mind helps us to understand difficult subjects like culture and religious experience. Culture is not something added to the personality, such as a knowledge of books, music, pictures, or plays. The attendants at art galleries, concert halls, and theatres can be very familiar with their subjects without being cultured people. The first requisite is harmony between the conscious and the unconscious minds. Cultured people are quiet and serene. They are not fighting down fierce temptations with a strong will. They have learned to use the unconscious mind.

It is a secret which every intellectual man quickly learns, that beyond the energy of his possessed and conscious intellect he is capable of a new energy (as of an intellect doubled on itself), by abandonment to the nature of things; that beside his privacy of power as an individual man, there is a great public power on which he can draw, by unlocking, at all risks, his human doors, and suffering the ethereal tides to roll and circulate through him; then he is caught up into the life of the Universe, his speech is thunder, his thought is law, and his words are universally intelligible as the plants and animals.[26]

Emerson sees such men travelling happily in the Stream of Life, at home with their fellow travellers, and not trying to set their own little wills against the will of God or Nature.

In II Timothy 2.24, we read, "The servant of the Lord must not strive; but be gentle unto all men, apt to teach, patient." This does not mean, of course, that he should subdue his own personality and drift through life without making a contribution to it. We are all in the world as new personalities, equipped to achieve some purpose, and nature has given each of us a strong egoism to enable us to get our work done, just as she has provided a strong sex instinct so that her latest creations shall not die out. The cultured man does not subdue that egoism. He refines it, so that he can use it in harmony with the egoisms of other people, who have also work to do in the world. The cultured man does not cut himself off from "the great world of God's cheerful, fallible men and women." He feels with Emerson that "These are not the best, but the best that could live in the existing state of soils, gases, animals and morals; the best that could yet live: there shall be a better, please God."[27] Is this not the outlook of our first-class teachers? They have communed with noble minds, found their place in the world, and know the beauty of it. They want to help in the melioration which is taking place in mankind; to increase the number of cultured people, and decrease the number who live from hand-to-mouth and never realize the greatness that is in them.

Children who are brought up by good teachers in this

kindly way not only learn more but they learn to take
hold of the problems of life by the right handle, as it were.
Think, for example, how differently people conduct a
discussion; one arouses antagonism immediately and the
discussion is fruitless, another knows that there are two
sides to most questions. He meets an extremist on what
common ground there is, as God sends the rain on the just
and the unjust. He holds his views quietly, and expresses
them in phrases that sing of love and not of hate, and his
opponent pays as much attention to the tune as to the
words, and is grateful for it. The cultured man tries to
speak to the other's *meaning*, not necessarily to the actual
words used. Scoring dialectic points does not interest him.
He wants to understand, and help if he can.

There is a noticeable *atmosphere* in the classroom of a
first-class teacher which is explained by one of Freud's discoveries (1915). "It is very remarkable that the *Ucs.* [un-
conscious mind] can react upon that of another without
passing through the *Cs.* [conscious mind]."[41] Good teachers seem to know this intuitively. They move about the
classroom as if every step matters. Their silence is as elo-
quent as their speech. Psychoanalysts who do not get the
right atmosphere with their patients have little success in
treating them, and the most skillful teaching can fall on
deaf ears if the unconscious minds of the teacher and
pupils have not met and flowed together. Education is an
unfolding. The whole history of mankind is in the unconscious minds of all of us. As Freud (1915) wrote:

> It is otherwise with the development of the mind. Here one
> can describe the state of affairs, which has nothing to compare
> with it, only by saying that in this case every earlier stage of
> development persists alongside the later stage which has arisen
> from it; . . . the primitive mind is, in the fullest meaning of the
> word, imperishable.[42]

[128]

We read good books and study art and music *in order to evoke our own powers*. We must not let books overrule us. We must not run to books or pictures or music to get away from the ugliness of life. If we are men we shall try to tidy up some of the ugliness. The cultured man knows of our rich inheritance. If he does not see "the conscience, the better the 'nobler' impulses"[38] in another, he will think, with Freud, that they are in the unconscious and have not been evoked. If he can help to evoke them, he will. And how near this outlook is to the teaching of the prophets and to the principles that Jesus taught!

The Limitations of the Intellect

Man has so much more intellectual power than the animals that at one time there was a tendency to think animals acted in a mechanical way by instinct, and man acted by a superior faculty called reason. The poets, artists, and musicians did not take this view. Plato said that "poets utter great and wise things which they do not themselves understand"[24] and the creative artists have always told us they depend largely on what is very like an outside power for their achievements. It was Freud, however, who first made it clear to us, that while our intellectual power is important, it is very ineffective unless it has access to our instinctive power. There is a lot more to our brain than a cerebral cortex, and much human wisdom is associated with the older parts of the brain.

"Don't confuse me with the facts," said the chairman of a large scientific organization. He wanted his unconscious mind to have a look at the problem, for although the facts may have been correct, he had "a hunch" that the line of approach chosen may not have been the best one. Scientists work more often from "a hunch" than from the "scientific method" of collecting the facts, arranging the facts,

[129]

putting forward a hypothesis to account for the facts, and using this hypothesis to make predictions. That method can be used by the intellect alone without instinctive backing, but if so used, it does not often produce results of importance. Think of Welsbach, looking for a new filament for the electric globe, and because of a bright speck on his bunsen burner, changing his research, and discovering the gas mantle instead. Or of Fleming, seeing a spot on one of his culture plates, and by concentrating on that accident, discovering penicillin.

Freud has shown us that the intellectual processes are largely at the mercy of an unconscious mind, most of which is inherited. The unconscious mind contains the "good" qualities which make the saint, the scientist, the artist, and other desirable citizens, and the "bad" qualities of the wolf, the monkey, and the savage; so that for all practical purposes we are back with God and the devil again, whether we like it or not.

As the distinguished physicist, Sir Edward Appleton, once said, "Science has brought back into life the mystery that at first it seemed to take out of it." In Luke 17:21, we find that Jesus said, "The kingdom of God is within you," and all the prophets realized that the devil was within us too. In I Peter 5:8, we read, "Be sober, be vigilant; because your adversary the devil, as a roaring lion, walketh about, seeking whom he may devour." This is a symbolic statement of the advice many a wise modern parent gives to one of his children leaving the protection of the home for the first time.

When I first went to East London as inspector of schools, I found some infants schools, often in very poor buildings, giving such splendid education that I had never seen anything to compare with it in the hundred schools I had visited previously, and these included some of the most famous Public Schools. The Heads and staffs had the missionary spirit, and had organized their work by their maternal instinct, and the maternal instinct can be very wise and very clever. Of all educational theorists, Froebel has had the most beneficial influence in the schools, and his advice to teachers was to teach as a mother teaches. After all, even in the animal kingdom mothers know a lot about how to bring up their young. There is much less of this maternal approach, however, when pupils leave the infants school. The teaching tends then to become intellectual in character, and unfortunately, often intellectual without instinctive support. For this reason much of it is superficial and a waste of time.

Freud (1923) wrote, " . . . I cannot make any use of ideas that are suggested to me when I am not ready for them."[30] But do we not all feel more or less like this when we have got rid of our teachers? The knowledge and wisdom which cultured people have has *grown* on them. It has not been *stuck* on. Now why don't we allow knowledge and wisdom to grow on children? In all schools except Grammar Schools it could be done quite easily, and even in Grammar Schools the approach could be tried in the lower forms.

Overemphasis on intellectual processes has another bad effect; it is partly responsible for the drift away from a religious outlook on life. The intellect in itself is not a satisfactory guide to the good life. Darwin described himself as an agnostic, but he went to church regularly and he was not a hypocrite. Freud was also an agnostic, and did not go to church, but he wrote (1924), "My deep engrossment in the Bible story (almost as soon as I learnt the art of reading) had, as I recognized later, an enduring effect upon the direction of my interest."[49] The Swiss pastor, Oskar Pfister, who knew Freud very well, said of him (1918), "A better Christian there never was."[39]

If the symbolism of the Bible were taught as symbolism, children would understand it better. Children are familiar with symbolic language. The dreams of young children are often full of symbolism, and they use it frequently in everyday speech. One of my children said, for example,

> There were so many buses, they were running along like a current of water.

> The way you get your salary is just like a bridge, isn't it Daddy? "How's that John?" Well, you go a long time without support. [I was a university lecturer at the time, and was paid three times a year.]

> I can't understand how God was made. Do you know what I believe? God is just a memory, a lot of plans, living plans, all the plans we'd better do. [Age, one day less than six years old.]

The children could be told that the story of the creation of the world, given in two different versions in Genesis Chapter I and Chapter II, was an old poetical description of the origin of the world. They could be told that the story of Jonah and the great fish was a story with a meaning, like the story of the Good Samaritan or the Prodigal Son. Jonah and the great fish are symbols, not historical facts. When Jesus said (Luke 17:6), "If ye had faith as a grain of mustard seed, ye might say unto this sycamine tree, Be thou plucked up by the root and be thou planted in the sea; and it should obey you," what Jesus meant was that if we had faith we could do wonders. Symbolism must not be translated literally.

The temptations of Jesus are the temptations we all have to face from our internal devil, namely to turn the difficulties of life to our own advantage (stones into bread),

[132]

to do foolish and dangerous things in the hope that God would protect us, and to take sides with evil in order to enrich ourselves. The wisdom of the Bible, especially the teaching of Jesus, is so remarkable and so important for the good life, that it is a pity children do not know it better than most of them do nowadays. It is tragic to hear of young people who *thought* there was no harm in letting the devil in them have a run, and finding themselves alcoholics, or drug addicts, or enslaved by cigarettes.

I should recommend, therefore, that teachers should think less about the intellectual and logical approach in their teaching, and more about each child building knowledge and wisdom in his own way. To do this, the child must have means of expression. If a teacher has thirty or forty pupils, written expression is the only practical form. All children can write at once. They cannot all talk at once or make models at once. Writing an original book on geography, history, science, religion, or anything else, enables a child to select the parts of the subject which fit on to his own background. It will then take root and grow. I have seen many schools where this procedure is followed. They are all very good schools, with happy, well behaved children, and a high standard of work.

I want to reiterate one qualification; it takes experienced teachers to use free methods. I have never seen a teacher successful with free methods who could not teach easily and successfully by orthodox methods, and I should like to see all young teachers using orthodox methods first. This is much the easiest form of teaching. It is backed by suitable and carefully graded textbooks on every subject, and children are more easily controlled when they are sitting in desks than when they are free to wander about. There must always be some well disciplined class work or children don't get the quietness and serenity they need at times, and teachers become exhausted. I should like all training colleges to pay more attention to the technical skill in handling forty children in a class, even if less attention was given to the more general subjects.

Educational Therapy

The London Education Authority has at present 41 classes for children who are in need of special help. Each class is taken by a teacher, usually one who has no qualification in medicine or psychology, and has had no special training for this work. The number of children in each class is limited to four or five. In an educational system in which teachers are scarce, where classes are usually of thirty or forty pupils, and where there are special schools for the mentally handicapped, the partially sighted, and so on, these small classes are an anomaly, and began in a strange way. Their effectiveness throws considerable light on the value of the educational methods we have been advocating, and they have greatly interested some of the specialists in the therapeutic work with children.

In anticipation of the bombing of London, masses of children were evacuated to the country, most of them without their parents. Nowadays we understand better how such separation can cause alarming fears, and regression in social training. Enuresis, for example, became more common. Even when children are reunited with their mothers they can be very difficult, refusing to leave them, refusing food, or showing aggressive tendencies which are difficult for the parents to control. As there was no bombing for a time, many parents and children returned to London. When bombing began, many were evacuated again, and there was considerable movement of this kind. The teachers, of course, were sent with the children, or after them.

One day Dr. Holman, the psychiatrist at The London Hospital, came to see me, the inspector of schools for the District, and asked if we could help her to cope with the many difficult children who were reporting for treatment. Some of them would not go to school because they could not read, and ability to read was assumed at their ages. If we would teach reading the clinic would try to cure the delinquency, enuresis and other difficulties.

The headmistress of an infants school, Mrs. Davids, had just returned for duty in London, and as her London school had been bombed, I asked her if she would help these children. She agreed to do so, and we used a spare room in the Care Committee office. She had five pupils. She not only taught them to read very quickly, but, to the surprise of all of us, the enuresis and delinquency were also cured in most cases *without* special treatment. This was a thrilling success, and we added another child to the group. To our surprise, she found six were too many. The tone of the class had collapsed. This first-class teacher, who could handle any ordinary class of forty infants, or conduct a school of four hundred, could manage five difficult children, but not six. So we kept the number at five. As they learned to read and were cured, they returned to their own schools, and made way for others. When a place for half a day became vacant in the small class, another pupil was taken for half a day. If he needed more, as he usually did, he got it as soon as possible. Most of the pupils came part time so that they did not lose contact with their own school.

About this time, the Case Conference was inaugurated. Several clinics for difficult children had been set up in London under private arrangements, and as they were treating some London schoolchildren, they asked for financial assistance from the London Education Authority.

Grants of £50 soon had to be increased to larger sums, and some effective control over this expenditure was administratively necessary. The Case Conference had to help in this control. It consisted of the district inspector (chairman), the divisional officer, the medical officer for the Division, and the organizer of children's care. In East London we included the teacher in charge of the small class. All difficult children were referred to this committee, which would advise head office on treatment, and payment would only be made for such treatment as was officially approved.

In East London, the Case Conference proved remarkably useful. Heads of schools, parents, doctors, clergymen, and others, brought to our notice children who were in need of help of some kind, and the Case Conference team considered every case. Some were aggressive or could not learn. Some were undernourished and were sent to open air schools and given extra food. Some were found to be with a difficult teacher, and the inspector and headmaster arranged a change of class. Some were upset by the home environment, and the divisional officer or the Care Committee officer would see what could be done. But our great refuge was the small class, and we soon opened another one. This disturbed the Ministry of Education, for teachers were scarce. They agreed to let us carry on if we took 12 children in the class. As this arrangement was useless for our purpose we ignored the recommendation and carried on. It was war time, we were all doing good educational work in London amid the bombing, and the Ministry did not press us.

More small classes were soon required, and I interviewed a teacher who had trained as a psychologist, wanted to carry on as a psychologist, and would not accept an ordinary teaching post. She seemed a suitable person for the work, and would not raise difficulty with the Ministry of Education. She was appointed, was a failure, and gave it up. I interviewed another teacher who wanted such work, and was not available for class teaching. She was appointed and also failed.

We found that the most suitable person for the work was a good teacher who could handle a class of forty successfully. A good mother substitute, rather than a psychologist. The technical skill of the good class teacher is invaluable in the handling of five difficult children. For what wrecks the class of six is jealousy. The children could only be cured if there was a love relationship between the teacher and the pupils. If there was love, there was jealousy, and only a good teacher knew how to evoke the love without evoking the jealousy. But even good teachers can seldom maintain a strong love relationship and avoid a jealousy relationship if the numbers exceed five. Children who are already maladjusted can learn to accept a family number, not more. The work in the small class is rather like the work in the early stages of a good infants school; the teacher tries to find points of interest, and then encourages the development of these. In other words, she tries to free the unconscious mind and let it function. Then the difficult child becomes more normal, and can develop in a natural way. Free drawing is popular at first, but reading, writing, arithmetic, and other school subjects are taught as required.

Soon we needed four such classes to deal with our problem children (there were 20,000 school children in the Division), and it was found desirable to use some specialist help. Some of the problem children were dangerous. The great advantage of a teacher who could handle forty children effectively was her constant vigilance. She saw, or anticipated, a dangerous action and stopped it in time. All the children in the special class were seen as soon as possible by the school medical officer, but it was considered advisable to have them interviewed also by a qualified psychiatrist.

Dr. Bonnard and Dr. Frankl, who were working part time for the East London Child Guidance Clinic, undertook this work, and gave us all—administrators, teachers, parents, and others—the benefit of their reports and advice on the various children. Their psychoanalytic knowledge especially proved most valuable for all of us. We were also in a better position legally if any serious accident did happen. A few children were sent for special psychiatric help, but very few.

We discovered it was undesirable to hold the small classes in ordinary schools, unless a separate area was available. Two such classes in adjacent rooms are unsuccessful. One class tends to cause excitement or jealousy in the other. The children like a mother of their own, in a home of their own.

In the small classes, about fifty per cent of the children made great improvement and returned to normal schooling. The remainder went to special schools of various kinds. Only the striking success of these classes would have increased them to 41 in London, and more every year in other authorities.

As the success of the classes is due to evoking the inherited emotional life and powers of the children, allowing these to develop, and training them for social adjustment, teachers who maintain this happy atmosphere in their large classes are doing much more than giving their pupils knowledge. They are definitely building a better society.

Think of those of our adolescents, male and female, who are causing us some concern at present. How many of them enjoyed their school work? Is it not the case that for most of them their instinctive life was repressed in school, and information they did not want was offered to them day after day? Their instinctive drives, increased in force by puberty, have to get expression somehow, and in such circumstances the expression can only be at the primitive level.

Some Further References to the Unconscious Mind

The unconscious mind is not a simple subject, and I think it will help if, in conclusion, I give some further examples of how distinguished people have made use of it.

Let us look at the musicians first:

> Schubert is, indeed, the very type of the spontaneous musician. He sang as the lark sings, with the same abandon and exuberance. It is even on record that a week or two after composing a song he would fail to recognize it as his own when it was put before him.[74]

> We know the curious way in which the unconscious worked in Hugo Wolf—how he would read a poem and brood upon it over-night, but without making any attempt to translate it into music; and then sleep upon it and in the morning find that the music had made itself, and that so completely, with such unerring logic, that all Wolf had to do was to fix the notes upon paper as fast as his pen would let him.[69]

It appears then, that for Schubert and Wolf the unconscious mind does most of the work. Schubert wrote eight songs on one day (October 13th, 1815), and during that year he wrote 144.[75] The intellect cannot work at that pace. The ideas must have been pouring in at the gate. Music is related to human emotions, and Schubert's unconscious mind was full of inherited human emotions.

From his earliest years he had evoked this inherited richness in musical forms, and his mind went on creating
music whether he was thinking about it or not. Wolf
worked in the same way. He started his mind thinking
about suitable music for the poem, and it went on thinking about it while he was asleep. Beethoven, on the other
hand, had to do more conscious work with the material
which his unconscious mind presented to him.

> "You will ask me how my ideas come. I cannot tell you with cer-
> tainty. They come uncalled for—directly, indirectly, I can grasp
> them with my hands in the open air, in the woods, when walking
> in the silence of the night, in the early morning, excited by moods
> which the poet puts into words and I put into tones, tones which
> roar and storm around me until I see them at last in notes before
> me."[82]
>
> The agonies through which he [Beethoven] sometimes went in
> the composition of a work were the result of this terrific effort at
> condensation of the unconsciously previsioned whole into its con-
> sciously isolated germ—themes; once these had been formed they
> almost spontaneously regenerated the whole with comparatively
> little effort on his part.[70]

I have quotations to the same effect from Tchaikowsky,
Berlioz, and Brahms.

Acting provides another interesting example of the unconscious. Sarah Bernhardt wrote:

> Whatever I have to impart in the way of anguish, passion or
> joy comes to me during rehearsal in the very action of the play.
> There is no need to cast about for an attitude, or a cry, or anything
> else. You must be able to find what you want on the stage in the
> excitement created by the general collaboration. Actors who stand
> in front of a mirror to strike an attitude or try to fall down on
> the carpet of their room are fools. They will effect nothing at all
> this way. Everything must come from suggestion.[4]

And Gloria Swanson is quoted as saying:

> The subconscious plays a most important part in my work. When I am acting, I will do some piece of business without having any ideas that I am doing it. The producer will call out, "That's good, do that again." But I shan't have any idea what I did, and often I may not be able to do it again. That is why I know that I am a very difficult person to act with.
>
> I expect that you have heard that an actress becomes so absorbed in a part that she acts it off the stage as well as on. That is true of my work. When I was playing Sadie Thompson in *Rain* I became Sadie Thompson entirely. I forgot my manners, I came down to dinner looking exactly like her. I am told that I even talked like her. This isn't a pose or an attempt to appear "temperamental"; it merely happens to be a rather interesting fact.[71]

Sarah Bernhardt and Gloria Swanson *evoke* the emotional situations from their own unconscious minds. They have inherited the emotions of their ancestors, and by evoking and practicing certain of these they can portray them perfectly without thinking. Actors and actresses who can portray a variety of characters successfully tend to be people of labile character. People of stable character cannot do this; from the rich inheritance of possible behavior with which they began life, they have built up *one* character, and they do not find it easy to depart from it.

Let us look now at a few more of the writers. Schiller explains in one of his letters, which Freud quoted (1900), why a creative artist should not allow his intellect to interrupt the flow of inspired thought.

> The ground for your complaint seems to me to lie in the constraint imposed by your reason upon your imagination. I will make my idea more concrete by a simile. It seems a bad thing and detrimental to the creative work of the mind if Reason makes too close an examination of the ideas as they come pouring in— at the very gateway, as it were. Looked at in isolation, a thought

may seem very trivial or very fantastic; but it may be made important by another thought that comes after it, and, in conjunction
with other thoughts that may seem equally absurd, it may turn
out to form a most effective link. Reason cannot form any
opinion upon all this unless it retains the thought long enough
to look at it in connection with the others. On the other hand,
where there is a creative mind, Reason—so it seems to me—
relaxes its watch upon the gates, and the ideas rush in pell-mell,
and only then does it look them through and examine them in a
mass. . . .[33]

We have seen how Darwin learned not to interrupt the
flow of inspired thought (p. 43) and here is more from
John Galsworthy telling how he created his novels:

> Mr. John Galsworthy criticised the modern novel when he de-
> livered the Romanes lecture on "The Creation of Character in
> Literature" in the Sheldonian Theatre today. As one "who has
> been trying to write novels of character over a period of more than
> thirty years," he gave an inkling of how he goes about it.
>
> "The vitality and freedom of character creation derives, as a
> rule," he said, "from the subconscious mind instinctively supplying
> the conscious mind with the material it requires. In attempting an
> illustration of that process you must forgive my being personal
> for a moment.
>
> "I sink into my morning chair, a blotter on my knee, the last
> words or deed of some character in ink before my eyes, a pen in
> my hand, a pipe in my mouth, and nothing in my head. I sit. I
> don't intend; I don't expect; I don't even hope. I read over the
> past pages. Gradually my mind seems to leave the chair and be
> where my character is acting or speaking, leg raised, waiting to
> come down, lips opened ready to say something. Suddenly my pen
> jots down a movement or remark, another, another, another, and
> goes on doing this, haltingly, perhaps, for an hour or two. When
> the result is read through it surprises one, by seeming to come out
> of what went before, and by ministering to some sort of possible
> future."[12]

Let us consider now what the scientists have to say.
Benzene was the first substance the chemical structure of

which was represented by a closed chain of atoms and not by an open chain. During the course of a Chemical Society Memorial Lecture, Francis R. Japp quoted Kekulé as follows:

I was sitting, writing at my textbook; but the work did not progress; my thoughts were elsewhere. I turned my chair to the fire and dozed. Again the atoms were gambolling before my eyes. This time the smaller groups kept modestly in the background.

My mental eye, rendered more acute by repeated visions of the kind, could now distinguish larger structures of manifold conformation; long rows, sometimes more closely fitted together; all twining and twisting in a snake-like motion. But look! What was that? One of the snakes had seized its own tail, and the form whirled mockingly before my eyes. As if by a flash of lightning I awoke; and this time also I spent the rest of the night in working out the consequences of the hypothesis.[61]

In the same lecture we find:

Great as were Kekulé's powers as a thinker and investigator, it is no exaggeration to say that he was equally distinguished as a teacher, whether in the lecture room or in the laboratory. His speech was of extraordinary ease and precision. His lectures, which were delivered, so far as my recollection goes, without notes, might have been published in the form in which they were spoken.

Here is a description of how Elias Howe achieved his successful invention:

Up to this time all sewing was done by hand, and to Howe it occured that a machine might ease the housewife's burden. With an ailing wife and a small family, he worked night after night, after quitting the factory, at model after model; always defeated by trying to make the needle of the machine work as the ordinary needle works, with the eye in the head.

One night, after years of trial, he had a nightmare. He pictured himself as ordered by a savage king to make a sewing machine or die, saw himself a failure, and led out to death by executioners who carried spears through whose blades ran threads of sinew. That gave to his waking thoughts the key to the problem, for every machine needle has its eye at the point, not at the shoulder like ordinary needles.[11]

Professor W. H. Thorpe, F.R.S. says,

If we look through the list of recent Nobel prizewinners it becomes obvious that many, perhaps a large majority, achieve this by great leaps of imaginative insight; leaps which at the time they were made, may have had very little experimental or observational basis. . . .

In some respects therefore, many of the most important theories in the history of science are arrived at as much by the modes of thought of the artist and the pure mathematician as by those popularly considered to be characteristic of scientists.[81]

Sir Peter Medawar F.R.S., Director of the National Institute for Medical Research, said in a lecture given on the B.B.C. on September 4, 1967: "Intuition is the mainspring of all scientific action," and Freud (1887-1902) wrote, "We cannot do without men with courage to think new things before they can prove them."[31] Writing of Goethe and Helmholtz, Freud (1900) said, ". . . . what is essential and new in their creations came to them without premeditation and as an almost ready-made whole."[34]

There is no question, then, that we have great powers within us apart from our intellectual powers. All normal school children, even the dull ones, have these powers. How teachers can make use of them to improve the education in the schools has been the theme of this book.

Appendix

Freud's Influence on Education

When we were young teachers we were always being reminded that to teach John Latin it was necessary to know, not only Latin, but John. The remark was usually a prelude to explaining to us the need to study psychology, and many of you, like myself, labored through Stout's *Manual* and other heavy tomes and were disappointed to find that we knew no more about John at the end of it all than we did at the beginning. I remember being relieved when Dr. Bernard Hart, from whom I did learn something about the human mind, described Stout's psychology as "an excellent exposition of how you think you think."

Freud's work is different. It has thrown light on every aspect of my professional work, it has helped me in my relationships with my family and my colleagues, it has helped me to understand and appreciate literature, art and music, religion and love, and it has brought happiness and serenity into my life.

Freud's discoveries are difficult to understand at first. For two years after I had heard of them I could not accept them. His views seemed so illogical and so improbable. When I tried to argue with some of those who were con-

Presidential address delivered at the Annual Conference of the National Association of Inspectors of Schools and Educational Organizers, October 8, 1949.

verted I seemed to get no satisfaction. One would make a statement, and I would point out that my experience showed the exact oppposite to be the case. He would then ask if I did not see that that proved his point. I did not realize then that the logical, intellectual outlook tends to make one blind to simple human psychology which the common people accept as obvious. "Sometimes I love you, sometimes I hate you, but when I hate you it's 'cause I love you," sings someone, and any East End adolescent school-girl considers such behavior perfectly natural. I might have swallowed that point, but when self-assertion was explained as shyness, and horror of cruelty related to the wish to be cruel, I could not believe it.

I was told that the key to Freud's work was the interpretation of dreams, so I started on that subject. I soon found, of course, that many children's dreams are wish-fulfillments. They dreamed of having lots of sweets, of being at a party, of getting a penny from a kind lady, and so on. One dreamed that the school burned down, one that the teacher was run over by a tram, and one that the new baby was drowned in the bath. I knew enough of schools and new babies not to be surprised. Then a woman told me of a dream which she said was obviously not a wish-fulfillment. She had dreamed that her husband was dismissed from his job. If this happened in reality she would be in poverty at once. But when I learned that the husband was a sea-going engineer who only got home once in three months, and that she was always lamenting his absence, I was not so sure about it. My sister-in-law dreamed that she was back at school and doing brilliantly; all the teachers were very pleased with her. Actually she had done badly at school, had been called the dunce of the family, and was very hurt about it. I collected over two hundred dreams of this kind, analyzed some of them by

Freud's technique, and found the rich new world of the unconscious mind. I read in Isaiah, "And it shall even be as when an hungry man dreameth, and behold, he eateth; but he awaketh, and his soul is empty: or as when a thirsty man dreameth, and, behold, he drinketh; but he awaketh, and, behold, he is faint, and his soul hath appetite" (29:8), and I found dozens of similar references in literature. I began to understand the wish-fulfillment idea.

Some of the dreams which first aroused my interest in the unconscious mind are published in *Dreams and Education*[55] but it would take too much space to give them here. I shall mention only one. I dreamed I was at the wedding of a girl friend of mine, Mlle. Coffinier, in France. A simple wish-fulfillment, I thought, until I analyzed it and found I was the bridegroom in the show. In other words, I wanted to marry the girl myself. I was amused and told my wife. She said quietly, "I always knew you had a soft side for that girl." Now the interesting point is that I did *not* know this, and yet it was true. I had read and spoken French to this woman teacher on many occasions during the first World War, and she would not accept payment. I had asked my wife to send her a present and a letter, and I sent the address. My wife lost the address, sent the present and the letter to me, addressing the girl as "Chère Mlle. Chiffonier." It was as if she said "Dear Miss Chest-of-Drawers—Dear Miss Chiffon—Dear Miss Little-Bit-of-Fluff, How dare you interest my husband." All this was contained in a slip of the pen *of which my wife was unaware.*

Freud found that most dreams are witty in this way, and so he set out to investigate wit. He found that this too was a product of the unconscious mind, and published his views in "Jokes and their Relation to the Unconscious" (1905).[36] He explained that to speak of an old man who is very reminiscent as being "in his anecdotage," or to speak of the Christmas Holidays as "the alcoholidays," is exactly the kind of thing the dream does. If, for example, one dreams of Southton, it may stand for Southport and Brighton, where two similar incidents occurred. I feared once that I had offended two friends, one in the North and one in London. I dreamed I was having a happy *tête-à-tête* tea with the one, but he was leaning forward just like the other; I was friendly again with both.

The dream is a release of unconscious pressure; so is the funny story. Young children are trained away from their interest in bodily functioning and so they tend to be amused by stories of bodily functioning. If these interests are not gathered up by means of play with water, sand, clay, and paint, and steered into socially useful channels, the children will still as adults be very amused by stories of this kind. We all have friends with this little weakness. Adolescent boys soon become interested and amused by sex stories, for obvious reasons, and as most people have inhibitions of some kind about sex, such stories have a wide popularity. Notice, however, what remarkable insight one has into the character of a person by listening to what he regards as a funny story. He lays his unconscious mind bare without knowing it. His laughter shows the release of innermost feelings. Let us consider a few stories as examples.

"We have here in the studio Mr. A., who has a poultry farm in Surrey. He began it only two years ago and has already made a thousand pounds. He is going to tell us about it. Mr. A. . . ." Mr. A began, "The Announcer has made three small mistakes which I should like to correct before I go on. First, my poultry farm is not in Surrey, it's in Sussex. And it wasn't one thousand pounds, it was two thousand pounds, and I didn't make, I lost it."

When we first hear of this clever lad we feel very humble. We have tried to keep hens ourselves and the eggs cost us at least 1s. each. Or we have tried in other ways to make a thousand pounds and always failed. And we listen humbly to the great man. When he tells us it was not *one* thousand pounds but *two* thousand pounds, we feel even more of a worm before him; but when we hear he *lost* it, all our poor repressed self jumps with joy and strides confidently about the world again. We are more of a man than he is anyway.

A young man was left £20,000 and in three years found himself in the Bankruptcy Court. Asked what he did with the money, he said, "Well, some of it went on wine, and some of it went on women; and I'm afraid some of it was wasted."

Most men have spent money on alcohol and on entertaining their lady friends, but as a rule they do not talk freely about such expenses. This young man, whose extravagance was so much more than ours, talks as if such expenditure were a necessary part of his education, and our humble ego can throw out its chest again.

You will notice two of the essentials of a good story: the atmosphere should be such as to stir up some unconscious feeling, and the release of the feeling should be sudden and unexpected. When the conjurer began his performance by saying, "Ladies and gentlemen, I have performed this trick in front of the Prince of Wales, the Duke of York, and other well-known public houses," we see how cleverly he stirs up our inferiority complex and lets it have a run. Another example of the same type is the story of the Scottish minister of the last generation.

"And when you are down there burning in hell, the Lord in his infinite mercy will look down on you and pity you. And you will say, 'Lord, Lord, we didna ken, we didna ken.' And the Lord, in his infinite mercy, will say, 'Well, ye ken noo!' "

The preacher, with his intoned speech and Biblical phrases, stirs up our early religious training, awakens our hidden feelings of guilt about our shortcomings, makes us, as it were, humble ourselves before goodness, and then suddenly lets us see that he is less charitable and more spiteful than even we are.

> The shipwrecked mariner swam ashore and fell asleep exhausted on the warm sand. He wakened up to find a beautiful islander standing beside him. "Man want some clothes?" He did. She soon brought him some useful garments. "Man want some food?" He did, and she returned with excellent food, coconut milk, cigarettes and matches. When he was well fed and had his cigarette going she smiled at him and said, "Man like to play with me?" He looked up in surprise and said, "You don't mean to say you have a dart board too!"

Here we stir up repressions about sex, and have a vicarious satisfaction in someone else's interesting situation. Then we fear that the story is going further than we are prepared to tolerate and inhibitions come suddenly into play. We put the lid on the unconscious mind, so to speak. Then the innocent remark relieves all anxiety and our unconscious interests can express themselves. We are not all so shy about these things, of course. Many men are very pleased with the story because they feel they would not be such a fool as that sailor was.

Other stories depend for their effect on a frank portrayal of something we have unconsciously understood. "What oft was thought, but ne'er so well expressed," as Pope put it.[73] The man who lost his train walked slowly back, trying to control his annoyance. He saw a man stooping to tie his lace and pushed him over, saying,

"You're always standing there anyway." We all know this state of mind which someone has described as "going about like an accident looking for somewhere to happen." The pressure of early annoyance has been increased by a new incident and we must explode on something. "How can a man putt with those great liners sailing up and down?" has actually been said on a seaside golf course. One of the most amusing golf stories of this type is the following:

> The 12th hole had a stream in front of it. The talkative golfer described his morning round enthusiastically, "I had a beautiful drive at the 12th, chipped over the bonny wee burn, and sank my putt for a three." In the afternoon, when he had not played so well, he was heard to say, "I had quite a good drive at the 12th, but I put my second in that bloody ditch and took seven."

Now when we all behave more or less in these ways is it any wonder that some of us lack enthusiasm for the results of psychological investigations conducted by questionnaires? Have I a soft spot for Mlle. Coffinier? I answer honestly and truthfully, "No." Has my wife any jealousy about Mlle. Coffinier? She answers honestly and truthfully, "No." And we are both wrong. One of my uncles was a keen church worker. While putting up Christmas decorations for the Sunday School he fell off a ladder and broke his leg. The church sent one or two letters of sympathy, but left him to stand a serious financial loss. He has been a fierce opponent of all churches ever since. He does not know the reason for this and he has built up an excellent logical and scientific case for his views. Bernard Hart found a similar case—the scientific agnostic had really given up the church to which he was devoted because one of the Sunday School teachers had jilted him. Even *very good* reasons are not necessarily the *real* reasons.

We see the same things in literature. Wordsworth, writing of the daffodils, says, "A poet could not but be gay/in such a jocund company!"[86] But Herrick says, "Fair daffodils, we weep to see you haste away so soon."[54] It all depends on the poet's mood. Burns writes:

> Wee, modest, crimson-tipped flow'r,
> Thou's met me in an evil hour;
> For I maun crush amang the stoure
>   thy slender stem:
> To spare thee now is past my pow'r,
>   Thou bonnie gem.[6]

This has little to do with a daisy. When, the same evening, Burns was going out to meet one of his lady loves, one could picture him swishing the heads off daisies, dandelions, and anything else within reach of his stick, in sheer exuberance of spirit. For the moment the daisy touched his own complex. Let him talk freely around the idea as a psychoanalyst would encourage him to do and we shall soon get at the real trouble.

> Such is the fate of simple bard,
> On life's rough ocean luckless starr'd
> Unskilful he to note the card
>   Of prudent lore,
> 'Till billows rage, and gales blow hard,
>   and whelm him o'er.[6]

Shakespeare often wrote in a similar way. In *Hamlet*, for example, when Ophelia is returning his presents, Hamlet says:

> Get thee to a nunnery, go; farewell. Or, if thou wilt needs marry, marry a fool; for wise men know well enough what monsters you make of them. To a nunnery, go; and quickly too. Farewell. . . .

I have heard of your paintings too, well enough; God hath given you one face, and you make yourselves another: you jig, you amble, and you lisp, and nickname God's creatures, and make your wantonness your ignorance. Go to, I'll no more on't; it hath made me mad.[78]

These remarks are not at all appropriate for Ophelia as she is portrayed for us in the play. For the moment Shakespeare has forgotten his play. His pretend anger against Ophelia has stirred up his own real anger against, perhaps, the Dark Lady of the Sonnets, who *was* a minx. Hence, it would be better, I suggest, if Hamlet did not look so closely at Ophelia as Laurence Olivier does while he is making these remarks. Of course, the matter is deeper than that. Hamlet's love and hatred of Ophelia originated in his love and hatred of his mother. This is obvious in the play. He is in the depth of despair before he hears that his father was murdered. It was his mother's marriage that had upset him. His infantile jealousy had been stirred up again. His jealousy is very obvious in the interview with his mother later on in the play. Hamlet (Shakespeare) loved and hated his father and the dream mind divided this complex father into two persons: the perfect father, and the wicked father who sleeps with the mother (the uncle). Myths, and the literature of every country are full of this theme, and Shakespeare had many similar stories to draw upon.[63] In the *Odyssey* we have the perfect father, Ulysses, and the wicked suitors who want to sleep with the mother. This dream mind splitting of the complex figure is perhaps more obvious in Cinderella, where the mother is divided into two persons: a fairy godmother (as the mother was in the first year of the baby's life) and a wicked stepmother (as the mother became at times after that, when she had to correct and discipline the baby, and give some of her love to other members of the family).

This mother complex is a necessary part of the development of every child. Every child needs mother love if he is going to be a good citizen. Every boy, when an infant, should feel some jealousy and envy of his father if his masculine qualities are to be safely developed. We get a remarkable proof of this outlook in our classes for delinquent children. We have three of these classes in my district. We find that the cause of delinquency in a large proportion of our cases is the absence of a normal love relationship with a mother or mother substitute. Hospitals and nurseries are the worst offenders. It appears to need a very bad East End mother to be as bad for the child as the average good nursery. There seems to be no satisfactory substitute for this intimate love relationship, and our most successful method of curing delinquent children of any age is to give them as a mother substitute a teacher whom they can love, and to whom they can anchor themselves until they learn gradually how to deal with the world around them. As, however, a delinquent child is usually as jealous as a baby we cannot have more than five pupils in attendance at once. Sometimes even five is too many, but seven is always too many. No lover hates his rival in love so fiercely as a baby does.

We see then that the main stream of mental life goes on below the surface. Unless one uses the main stream one can create little or achieve little. We must accept our racial heritage and compromise with it. We must face up to our faults and acknowledge them, to ourselves at least, or they will soon master us. Let me give you an example. A boy of 11 was delinquent and could not read, and we put him under an excellent infants' teacher in one of our small classes. After some weeks his behavior had improved but he still could not read a word. Then his teacher made a remarkable discovery. He was telling other boys in the class what the words were, even difficult words. Meantime the psychiatrist had got the following case history from the child and his mother. The boy loved his mother and tried to behave as she wanted him to behave. She wanted him to be a nice boy who did not know anything about sex or the female body. Crowded accommodation, however, had let him learn a good deal. He shared a room with his sister, for example, and he knew a good deal about parental relationships. But, being a *nice* boy, he must not see what he did see and must not know what he did know, *and this had spread to reading.* When the repressed ideas were brought to the surface and the mother was told to modify her training, the boy learned to read easily and his behavior improved very much.

Now this will seem a rambling paper to many of you. Dreams, wit, funny stories, poetry, plays and delinquent children. I cannot, in my enthusiasm, resist trying to tell you of the extraordinary richness of Freud's wonderful discoveries and how they illuminate and integrate every aspect of human life. For example, the first movement of Brahms' Symphony No. 2, the second movement of his Symphony No. 4, his "Variations on the St. Anthony Chorale," the *Odyssey, Hamlet,* the "Mona Lisa" and "St. Anne," and Shakespeare's "Sonnet No. 31" all tell the same story. It is a story that the institution child cannot tell and does not understand, because although it is in his racial heritage he has not lived through it. And it is because he has not lived through it that he finds difficulty in adjusting himself to a civilized life. In conclusion, I shall try to indicate some of the lessons I have learned from Freud's work.

One should try to have an integrated personality. Don't hide part of yourself from yourself. Although it spoils the nice picture you would like to have of yourself, just put up with it. You are no worse than the rest of us. Don't be taken in by my nice dreams. I had to hunt through a hundred to get one or two the Association would print. Every incident you repress takes some of your mental power to keep it down and it soon pulls down many other things as well. Something happens later which reminds you of the incident, that must be kept down too. And so you go on through life throwing mental energy away and keeping more of it for this silly purpose of repression.

One should not set too high a standard for one's own conduct. As the judge said to the prisoner, "You should not have murdered your wife, you should have left her." Similarly, you should not have left her and broken up the home, you should have joined a club and spent some of your leisure time there if you were finding life too difficult, and so on. The point being that one should not seek refuge from a disharmony by getting into a greater disharmony. That is what happens if the unconscious mind is allowed to collect power. One of these days it will take control altogether; or you will waken up one day and feel you are someone else; your real self has never lived. All good living must be a compromise with one's racial heritage; with one's savage and animal ancestry.

One should not expect too high a standard from one's friends and from one's pupils. Learn a lesson from the notice outside an East End restaurant—"If your wife can't cook, feed here and keep her as a pet." I remember a nice-looking young married woman teacher asking to see me (her inspector) after school hours. I gave her an appointment at my office. She began in a tragic manner and with tears pouring from her eyes, "Oh, Mr. Hill, I am so sorry to trouble you about this but I don't know what to do. The headmaster is making advances to me." "Oh, that's nothing to worry about," I said cheerily. "We all tend to get a bit like that at times. It is quite simple, you just keep him off." Her face cleared. "Shall I tell my husband about it?" she asked later. "No, I shouldn't if I were you. Why make him jealous and cause trouble? Deal with the matter yourself, in a kindly way if you can; you don't know what emotional strain your headmaster may be under at the moment. I won't mention it at all unless you write to me again." And she dealt with the incident quite nicely. Similarly with the children, don't make an unnecessary fuss about their lying, stealing, cruelty, sexual play, and so on. Children have to be steered away from such practices, of course, but they will be troubled all their life with feelings of guilt and anxiety if the training is not carefully and sympathetically done.

All mental processes are like the reflex arc, there must be stimulus and response. If the foot tickles and we cannot scratch, or the throat tickles and we cannot cough, strain is set up. It is the same with the instincts. If one is subjected to a succession of little annoyances and cannot retaliate, strain is set up. Engaged couples frequently suffer from this heaping up of emotional potential. The opposite state of affairs is just as bad. Outflow of nervous energy without a stimulus exhausts the body: physical exercise of any kind done without a purpose, or masturbation. This knowledge is of great importance in the classroom. See that every lesson has a stimulus part and a response part.

All creative work is done by the unconscious mind. Poets, artists, and musicians, for example, have to keep their intellectual and critical faculties in abeyance while the unconscious mind creates. Those who can allow their unconscious minds to function freely, write and speak easily. Similes and metaphors spring spontaneously to their minds and their words arrange themselves, accom-

[157]

panied by just the right tune for the mood the words express. That is why many young children write so well. A proof reader sometimes changes, say, a two-syllable word to a three-syllable word in my script and puts my prose out of step, or he makes an alteration which completely changes the tune, and the tune was carrying more of my meaning than the words. There are a few such changes in my books and they jar on me every time I read them, although the changes may have improved the grammar or the strict accuracy of the statement.

Now in case some of my colleagues fear that Freud's work will undermine moral values, let me say this. Freud found after a time that he could not tell a lie; it just was not worth the trouble. Everyone who understands the unconscious mind soon finds that his own standard of behavior is very exacting. He has now to shoulder the responsibility for his mistakes, his forgettings, his unpunctuality, his unconscious snubs, his wicked dreams, and all his uncharitableness. With a knowledge of the unconscious mind it becomes much easier to adopt a true Christian attitude towards one's fellows. One feels in the stream of life, a glorious part of life, but such a little part of life, so full of faults, so much under the control of millions of ancestors who have set our reflexes, instincts, dreams, and conduct that the most one can hope to do is stand at the helm, like the captain of a ship in a storm, and try to steer a safe course between Scylla and Charybdis. But it is glorious fun to be on the bridge and steering, with courage and humility, rather than hiding away from life in the cabin or the fo'c'sle and pretending there is no storm and no danger.

References

(1) Ardrey, R. *The Territorial Imperative*. New York: Atheneum, 1966, p. 124.

(2) *Ibid.*, pp. 148-152.

(3) *Ibid.*, p. 143.

(4) Bernhardt, S. *The Art of the Theatre*. New York: Reprint House International. 1924, p. 167.

(5) Bunyon, P. *The Pilgrim's Progress*. New York: New American Library of World Literature, 1964, p. 9.

(6) Burns, R. To a Mountain Daisy. In: *English Prose and Poetry 1660-1800*, ed. O. Shepard & P. S. Wood. New York: Houghton Mifflin, 1934, p. 907.

(7) Burt, C. L. The Psychology of Art. In: *How the Mind Works*, ed. C. L. Burt. New York: Appleton-Century, 1934, p. 275.

(8) Cannon, W. B. *Bodily Changes in Pain, Hunger, Fear, and Rage*. New York: Harper, 1936.

(9) *Ibid.*, p. 247.

(10) *Ibid.*, p. 131.

(11) *Children's Encyclopedia*, ed. A. Mee. London: Educational Book Company, c. 1930, 9:5946-5947.

(12) *Daily Telegraph* (London). May 22, 1931.

(13) Darwin, C. *Autobiography*, ed. N. Barlow. New York: Harcourt Brace, 1959, p. 72.

(14) ——*The Descent of Man* (2nd ed.) London: John Murray, 1874, p. 871.

(15) *Ibid.*, p. viii.

(16) *Ibid.*, p. 141.

(17) Einstein, A. *Albert Einstein, Philosopher—Scientist*. The Library of Living Philosophers, ed. P. A. Schlipp. New York: Tudor, 1951, p. 17.

(18) Emerson, R. W. Poetry and Imagination (Veracity). In: *The Complete Works*, 8:27-28. Boston & New York: Houghton Mifflin, 1903-1921.

(19) ——*The Complete Essays and Other Writings*, ed. B. Atkinson. New York: Random House, Modern Library, 1940, p. 267.

(20) *Ibid.*, p. 201.

(21) *Ibid.*, p. 191.

(22) *Ibid.*, pp. 298-299.

(23) *Ibid.*, p. 124.

(24) *Ibid.*, p. 140.

(25) *Ibid.*, p. 381.

(26) *Ibid.*, p. 332.

(27) ——The Young American. In: *English Traits, Representative Men and Other Essays.* New York: Dutton, 1923, p. 363.

(28) France, A. *Pierre Nozière,* trans. J. L. May. New York: Dodd Mead, 1925, p. 110.

(29) Freud, A. *The Ego and the Mechanisms of Defense,* Rev. Ed. New York: International Universities Press, 1966.

(30) Freud, S. (1873-1939), *The Letters of Sigmund Freud,* ed. E. L. Freud, trans. T. & J. Stern. New York: Basic Books, 1960, p. 346.

(31) ——(1887-1902), *Origins of Psychoanalysis.* New York: Basic Books, 1954, p. 137.

(32) ——(1900), The Interpretation of Dreams. *Standard Edition,** 4 & 5. London: Hogarth Press, 1953.

(33) *Ibid.*, p. 103.

(34) *Ibid.*, p. 613.

(35) ——(1901), The Psychopathology of Everyday Life. *Standard Edition,* 6. London: Hogarth Press, 1960.

(36) ——(1905), Jokes and their Relation to the Unconscious. *Standard Edition,* 8. London: Hogarth Press, 1960.

(37) ——(1908), 'Civilized' Sexual Morality and Modern Nervous Illness. *Standard Edition,* 9. London: Hogarth Press, 1959, p. 202.

(38) ——(1909-1937), *Psychoanalysis and Faith:* The Letters of Sigmund Freud and Oskar Pfister, ed. H. Meng & E. L. Freud, trans. E. Mosbacher. New York: Basic Books, 1963, p. 126.

(39) *Ibid.*, p. 63.

(40) ——(1912-1913), Totem and Taboo. *Standard Edition,* 13. London: Hogarth Press, 1955, p. 158.

(41) ——(1915), Papers on Metapsychology. *Standard Edition,* 14. London: Hogarth Press, 1957, p. 194.

(42) ——(1915), Thoughts for the Times on War and Death. *Standard Edition,* 14. London: Hogarth Press, 1957, p. 285.

(43) *Ibid.*, p. 296.

(44) ——(1916-1917), Introductory Lectures on Psycho-Analysis. *Standard Edition,* 15 & 16. London: Hogarth Press, 1963.

(45) *Ibid.*, p. 199.

(46) *Ibid.*, p. 338.

(47) *Ibid.*, p. 361.

(48) *Ibid.*, p. 371.

(49) ——(1924), An Autobiographical Study. *Standard Edition,* 20. London: Hogarth Press, 1959, p. 8.

(50) ——(1927), The Ego and the Id. *Standard Edition,* 19:3-66. London: Hogarth Press, 1961.

* *The Standard Edition of the Complete Psychological Works of Sigmund Freud,* Translated from the German under the general editorship of James Strachey in collaboration with Anna Freud.

[160]

REFERENCES

(51) Graves, R. *On English Poetry*. New York: Knopf, 1922, p. 27.

(52) Hardy, A. *The Living Stream*. London: Collins, 1965, pp. 257-261.

(53) Hartmann, E. *The Philosophy of the Unconscious*, 1, trans. W. L. Coupland. London: Kegan Paul, Trench, Trubner, 1893, p. 279.

(54) Herrick, R. To Daffodils. In: *The Golden Treasury*, ed. F. T. Palgrave. London: Oxford University Press, 1936, pp. 91-92.

(55) Hill, J. C. *Dreams and Education*. London: Methuen, 1926.

(56) *Ibid.*, pp. 1, 6-7.

(57) ———Poetry and the Unconscious. *The British Journal of Medical Psychology*, 4 (2). Cambridge: The University Press, 1924.

(58) ———*The Teacher in Training*. London: George Allen & Unwin, 1935, p. 5.

(59) ———& Robinson, B. A Case of Retarded Mental Development Associated with Restricted Movements in Infancy. *The British Journal of Medical Psychology*, 10 (3). Cambridge: The University Press, 1930, pp. 276-277.

(60) Huxley, T. H. Science and Education. In: *Collected Essays*, 3. New York: Appleton, 1910, p. 414.

(61) Japp, F. R. Kekulé Memorial Lectures, 1897. In: *Chemical Society Memorial Lectures 1893-1900*. London: Gurney & Jackson, 1901, p. 106.

(62) Jennings, H. S. *Prometheus, or Biology and the Advancement of Man*. New York: Dutton, 1926, pp. 41 ff.

(63) Jones, E. *Hamlet and Oedipus*. New York: Norton, 1949.

(64) Koestler, A. *The Act of Creation*. New York: Macmillan, 1964.

(65) *Ibid.*, pp. 114 ff.

(66) Luce, G. G. & Segal, J. *Sleep*. New York: Coward-McCann, 1966.

(67) *Ibid.*, pp. 154-155.

(68) Maugham, S. *The Narrow Corner*. London: Heinemann, 1932, p. 181.

(69) Newman, E. *The Unconscious Beethoven*. New York: Knopf, 1970, pp. 138-139.

(70) *Ibid.*, p. 141.

(71) Nichols, B. *The Star Spangled Manner*. New York: Doubleday Doran, 1928, p. 60.

(72) Nietzsche, F. *Beyond Good and Evil*. London: George Allen & Unwin, 1967, No. 68, p. 86.

(73) Pope, A. Essay on Criticism. In: *English Prose and Poetry 1660-1800*, ed. O. Shepard & P. S. Wood. New York: Houghton Mifflin, 1934, p. 341.

(74) Scholes, P. *The Listeners' History of Music*, 1. London: Oxford University Press, p. 152.

(75) ———*Oxford Companion to Music*. New York: Oxford University Press, 1970, sect. 5, p. 968.

(76) Shakespeare, W. *A Midsummer Night's Dream*. Act V, Scene 1.

(77) ———*The Merchant of Venice*. Act III, Scene 3.

(78) ———*Hamlet*. Act III, Scene 1.

(79) Stevenson, R. L. *Across the Plains*. New York: Scribner's, 1892, pp. 247-249.

REFERENCES

(80) Thucydides. *Works*, 1, Speech of Archidamus, trans. B. Jowett. Oxford: Clarendon Press, 1881, p. 53.

(81) *Times* (London). January 25, 1969.

(82) Turner, W. J. *Beethoven: The Search for Reality*. London: J. W. Dent, 1933, p. 194.

(83) Wells, H. G. *Experiment in Autobiography*, 1. London: Gollancz, 1930, pp. 323-324.

(84) Wharton, E. *A Backward Glance*. New York: Appleton-Century, 1934. p. 203.

(85) Whyte, L. L. *The Unconscious Before Freud*. New York: Basic Books, 1960.

(86) Wordsworth, W. The Daffodils. In: *The Golden Treasury*, ed. F. T. Palgrave. London: Oxford University Press, 1936, p. 259.

Index

Acquired characters,
   inheritance of, 121-123
Activity methods, 5, 9, 10, 11, 12,
   29, 54, 55, 56, 68, 70, 73
   difficulties in using, 11, 30
Adrenalin, 108
Aggression, 49
Ambivalence, 53
Ancestors, inheritance from, 38, 48
Appleton, E., 130
Ardrey, R., 122
Arithmetic, 24, 65, 66
Art, 83
   value of visual imagery of, 84, 85
Astronomy, children's book on, 25

Baby, development of, 48, 49
Backwardness, caused by restricted
   movements, 110-111
Beethoven, L., 140
Benzene, discovery of formula, 143
Berlioz, H., 140
Bernhardt, S., 140, 141
Bernheim, H., 40
Blake, W., 41, 83
Bonnard, A., 138
Books, marking of, 113-115
Bragg, W., 79
Brahms, J., 140, 155
*British Journal of Medical Psychol-
   ogy*, 2
Bunyan, J., 42, 43
Burns, R., 152
Burt, C., 115
Butler, S., 37, 123

Canada, children's books on, 20
Cannon, W., 108-110
Caruso, E., 91
Case conference, 135, 136
Charcot, J., 40
Children
   delinquent, 154
   designs of, 8
   diaries of, 14, 67
   dreams of, 38, 39, 156
   learning of, 3; *see also* Learning
      and sub specific subjects
   innate differences among, 49
   repression and aggression in, 49
   -teacher relationship, 9-10
   training of in case of fire, 49
   use of symbolism by, 132
Clay, educational value of, 60, 61
Coffinier, M., 147
Compositions, children's, 5, 6, 7, 91,
   92, 93, 94, 95
Culture, 126-129

Davids, M., 135
Darwin, C., 43, 86, 121, 124, 131, 142
Delinquency, 154
Designs, children's, 8
Diaries, children's, 14, 67
Diderot, D., 50
Discipline, 34, 36, 116-121
Dolls, educational value of, 63
Dramatic work, 17
Dreams, 40
   children's, 146
   recent medical research on, 38, 39

Dreams and Education, 2, 147
Drugs, effect of, 39

Education, importance of the early
    years, 53
    Act of 1944, 77
    physical, 106-110
Educational visits, 14
Educational therapy, 134-139
Ego, and id, 2
    and defense mechanisms, 2
Einstein, A., 80
Ekstein, R., vii, 1
Eliot, G., 86
Emerson, R., 37, 43, 46, 47, 83, 104,
    106, 126, 127
Enuresis, 134
Environment, arrangement for chil-
    dren, 55, 56, 57
Eton school, 79

Fears, unconscious, 35
Fire, 49
France, A., 44
Frankl, L., 138
Freedom, importance of, 58
Freud, A., 1, 2, 4
Freud, S., 2, 3, 4, 37, 38, 39, 40, 44,
    45, 50, 51, 84, 85, 107, 121, 122,
    124, 128, 129, 131, 132, 141, 144,
    145, 146, 147, 148, 155, 158
Froebel, F., 131
Fry, E., 18, 19
Fry, R., 7

Galsworthy, J., 92, 142
Genesis, 132
Geography, 101-104
Gigli, 91
Glasgow University, 30
Goethe, J., 51, 144
Graves R., 92
Greenwood, U., 54, 87, 94, 95

Handwork, 110-112
Hardy, A., 123
Harrow school, 79
Hart, B., 145
Hartmann, E., 37

Helmholz, H., 144
Herrick, R., 152
Hill, J., 1, 2
History, 18, 104-106
Hogarth Press, 40
Holman, D., 135
Howe, E., 125
Howlett, C., 9, 30
Huxley, T., 34
Hypnosis, 40

Infants schools, 5, 6
Innate powers, 51
Instinctual behavior, 49
Intellect, limitation of, 129-133

Japp, F., 143
Jeffreys, M., 105
Jennings, H., 111
Jesus, 129
    temptations of, 132
Jung, C., 45

Kekulé, F., 41, 114, 143
King's College, 118
Koestler, A., 93

Lamarck, J., 121, 123
Learning, ways of, 55
Lectures, on Junior School Methods,
    8
Lecturing, university, 32
London, bombing of, 134
London County Council, 1, 5, 7
London Head Teacher, 4

Macbeth, 39
Mathematics, 95-100
Maugham, S., 126
Medawar, P., 144
Migration, of birds and fish, 122
Mind and intellect, 123-126
Montessori, M., 106
Motto, R., 1
Mozart, W., 41
Music, 28, 86-91

Newton, I., 114
Nietzsche, F., 37, 44

Notebooks, children's, 12, 13, 39
Nursery school, 51, 59

Odyssey, 53, 153
Ontogeny, 48

Parent, as supporting ego, 49
Pfister, O., 45, 132
Phylogeny, 48
Physical education, 106-110
Pilate, 39, 129
Plato, 38, 129
Poetry, and unconscious, 2
Poincaré, H., 41
Portia (Shakespeare), 8
Presence, good, 32, 35
Psychology, 35
Public Schools, 131
Public speaking, 26, 27
Punishment, 10
Puppetry, 17-29

Reading,
    teaching of, 64
    tests in, 15
Reflex arc, 157
Repression, 45
Richardson, M., 7

Sand, educational value of, 60
Schiller, F., 37, 141
Schools, effect of changes of staff,
    30, 71-73
Schopenhauer, A., 37
Schubert, F., 139
Science teaching, 80, 81
Sequence in learning, 73
Sexuality, infantile, 50

Shakespeare, W., 41, 152, 153, 155
Speech training, 16, 17; *see also*
    Public speaking
Spelling and punctuation, 7
Stevenson, R., 92
Stubbornness, 51
Sublimation, 46
Suprarenal glands, 108
Swanson, G., 141
Symbolism, 132

Tables, multiplication, 66
Tchaikowsky, P., 140
Teacher in training, 2, 3
Teaching, *see sub subject*
Teachers, value of good, 45, 46
Thorpe, W., 144
Thucydides, 125
Toilet training, 52
Transport, lessons on, 22, 23

Unconscious fear, 35
Unconscious mind, vii, 44, 139-144

Voice production, 90

Washing mania, 39
Water, educational value of, 60
Watt, J., 114
Wells, H. G., 96
Weismann, A., 121
Welsbach, von, C. A., 130
Wharton, E., 43
Whyte, L., 93
Wit, examples of, 148-151
Wolf, H., 139-140
Wordsworth, W., 151

Please remember that this is a library book,
and that it belongs only temporarily to each
person who uses it. Be considerate. Do
not write in this, or any, library book.

DATE DUE